# OSCAR PETERSON
## A Royal Wedding Suite

ISBN 978-1-4234-6778-6

HAL•LEONARD®
CORPORATION

7777 W. BLUEMOUND RD. P.O. BOX 13819 MILWAUKEE, WI 53213

In Australia Contact:
**Hal Leonard Australia Pty. Ltd.**
4 Lentara Court
Cheltenham, Victoria, 3192 Australia
Email: ausadmin@halleonard.com.au

Visit Hal Leonard Online at
**www.halleonard.com**

# London Gets Ready

## By Oscar Peterson

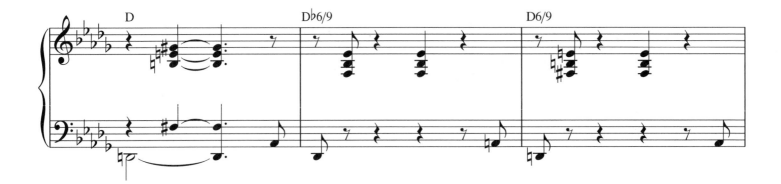

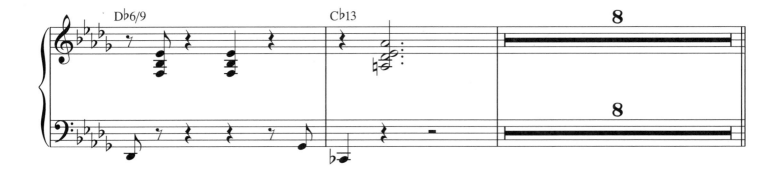

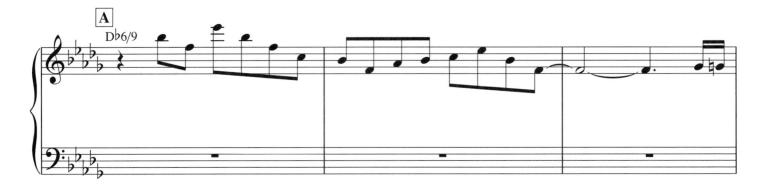

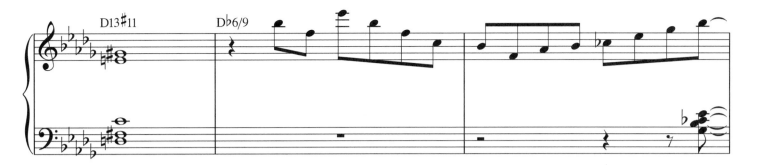

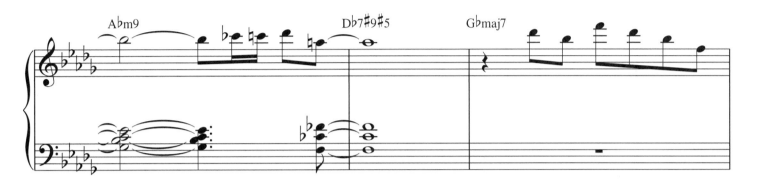

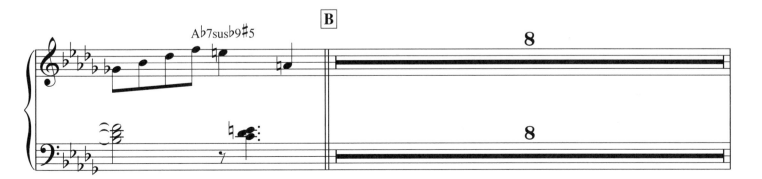

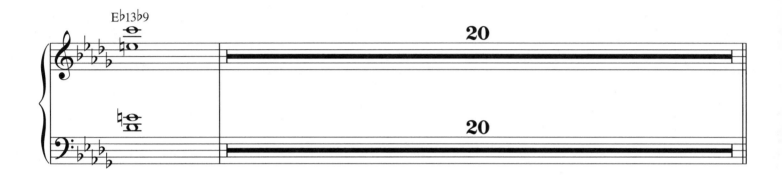

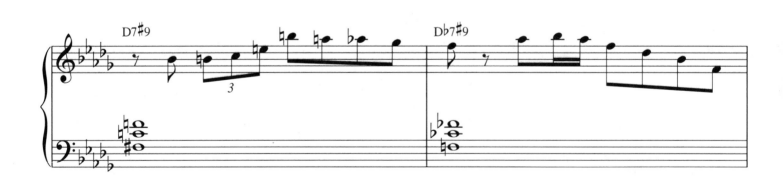

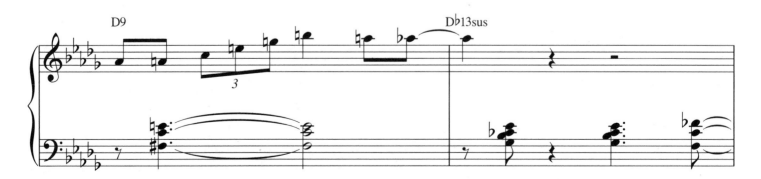

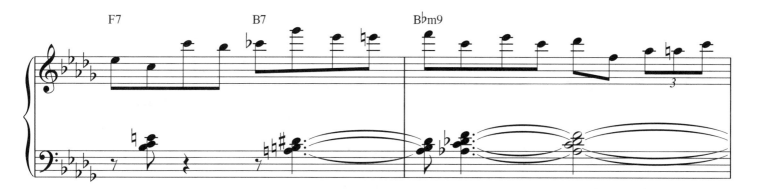

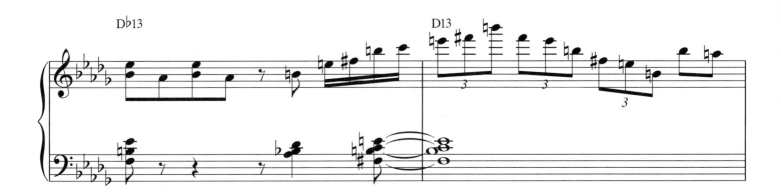

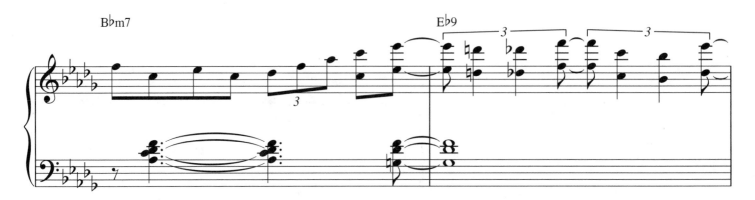

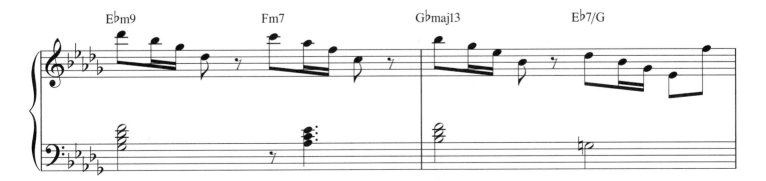

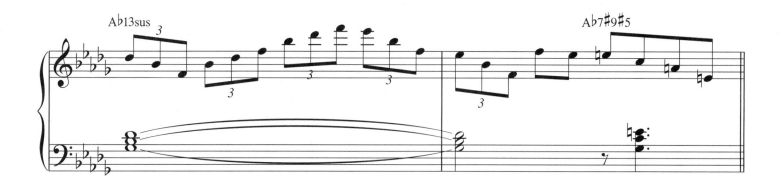

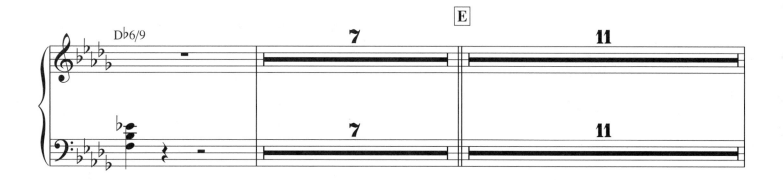

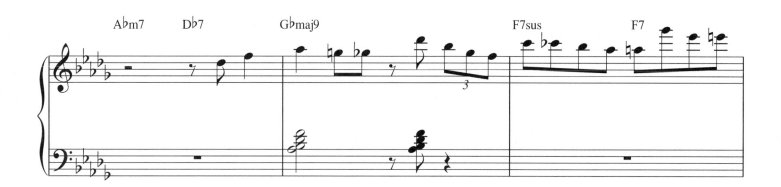

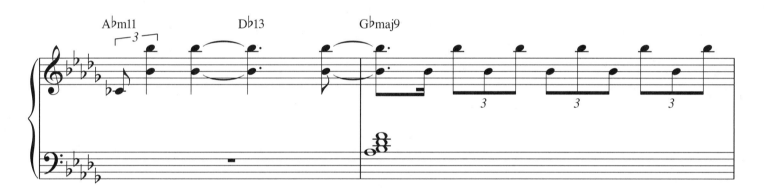

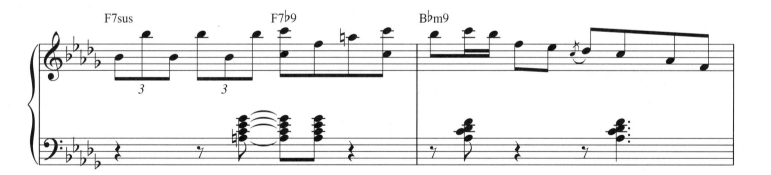

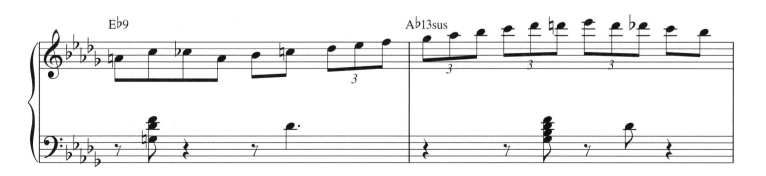

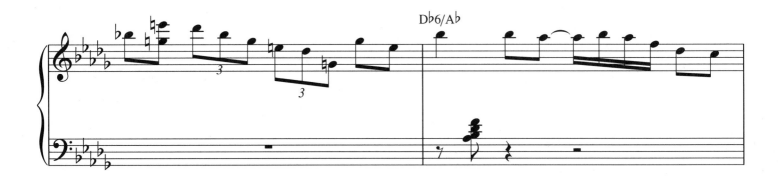

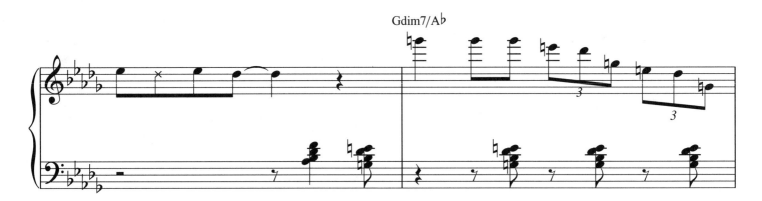

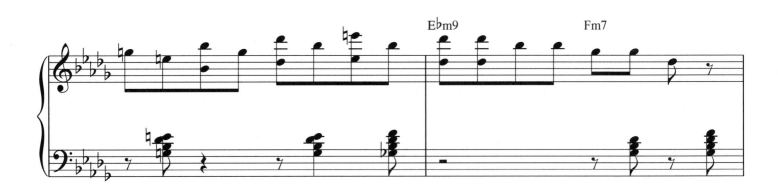

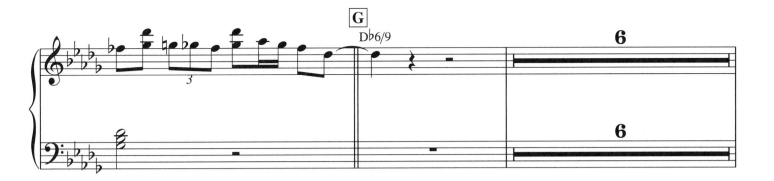

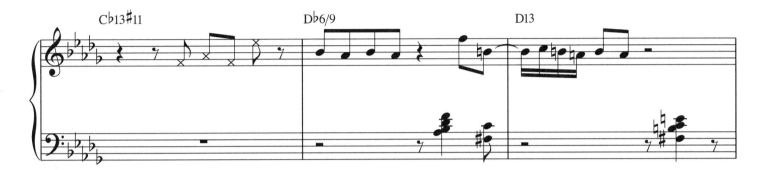

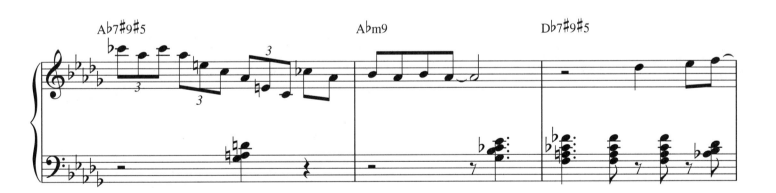

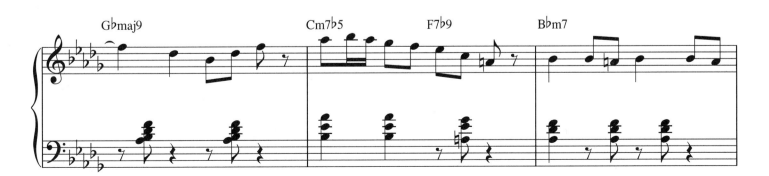

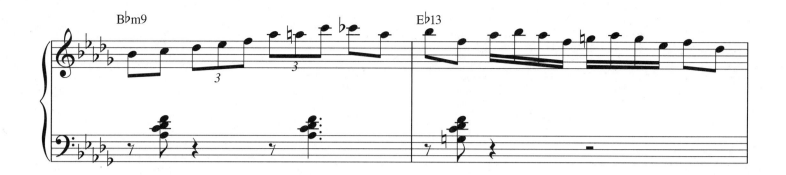

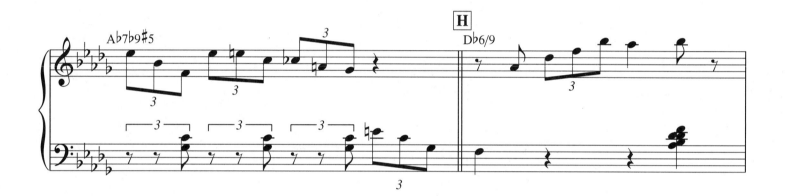

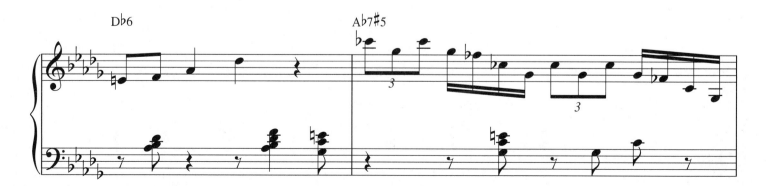

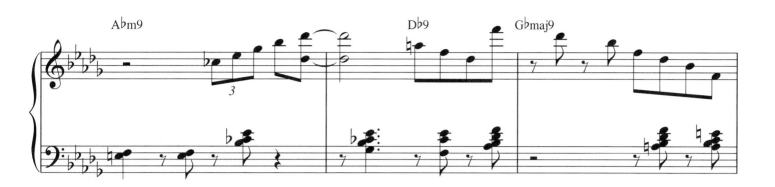

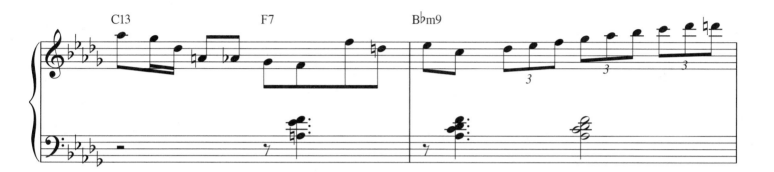

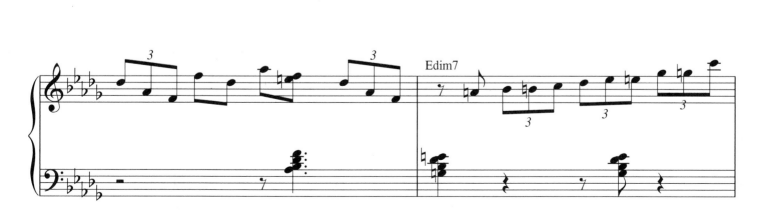

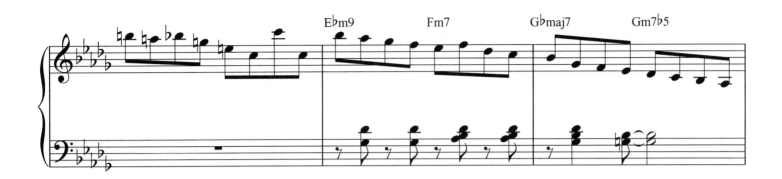

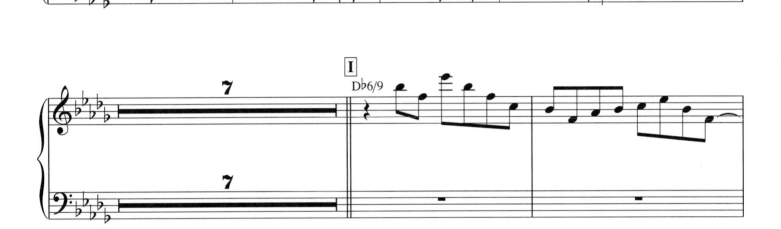

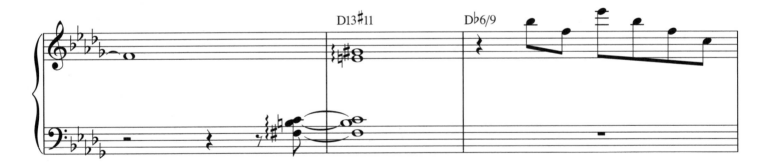

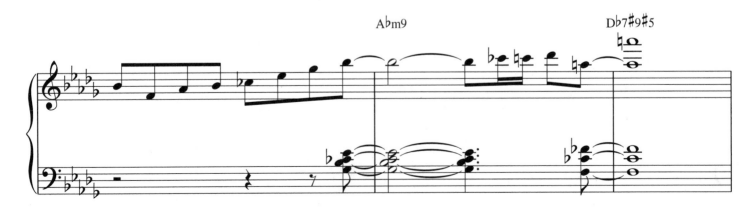

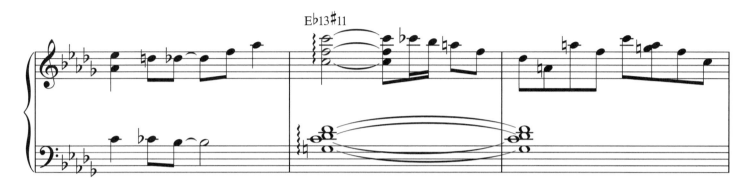

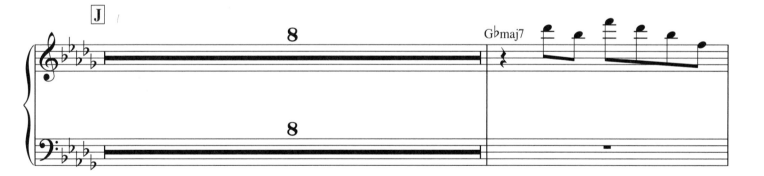

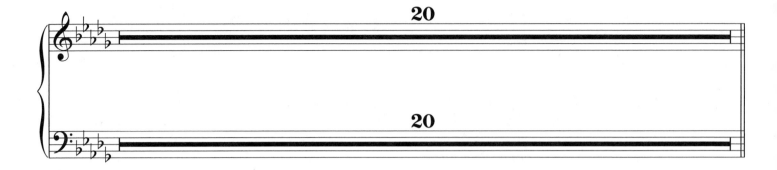

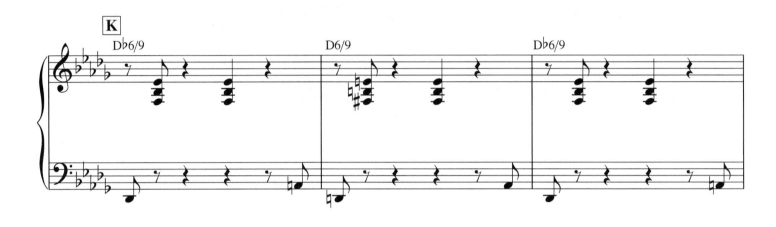

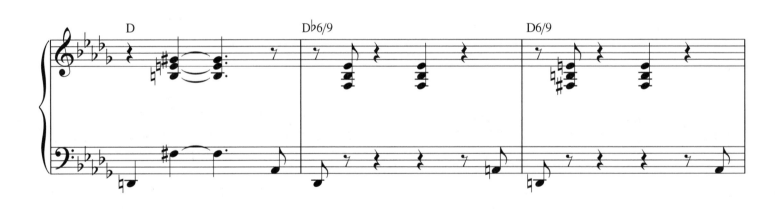

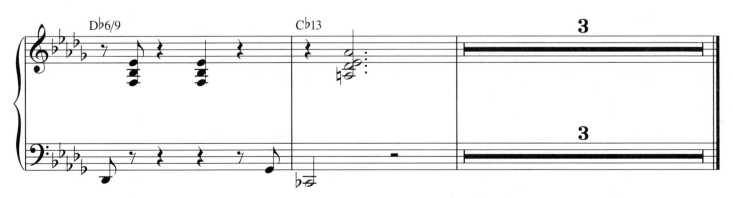

# When Summer Comes

## By Oscar Peterson

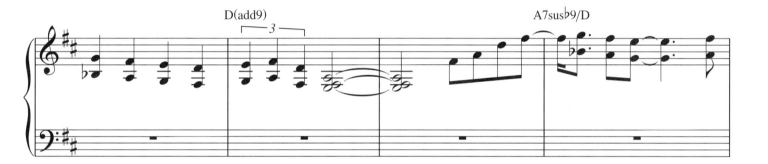

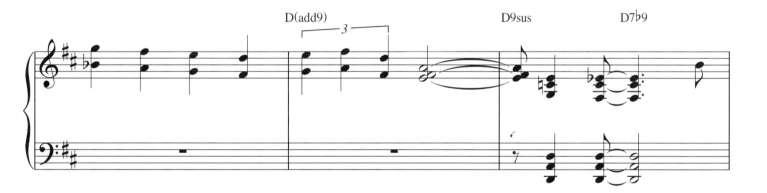

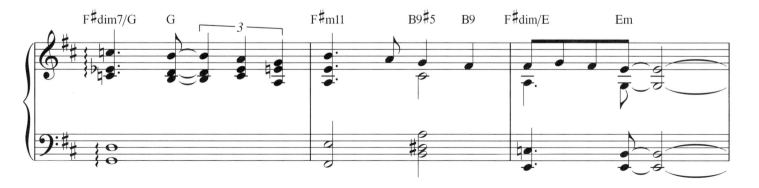

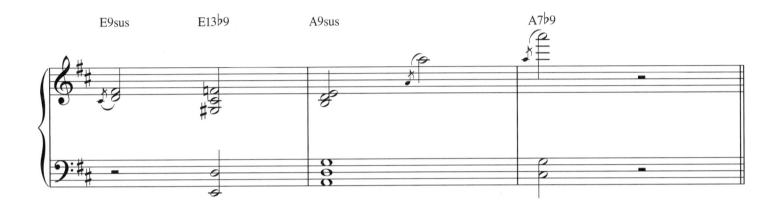

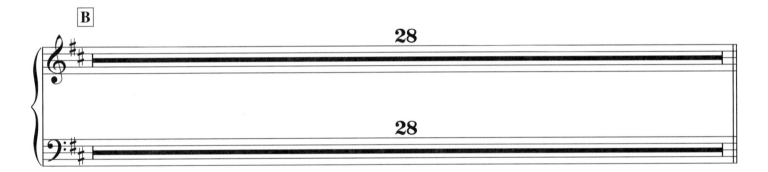

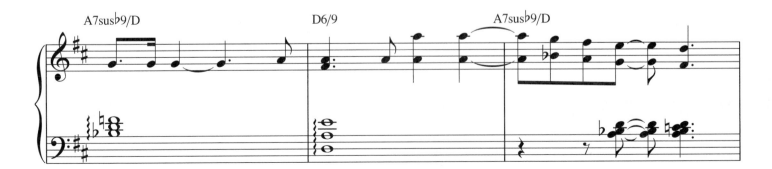

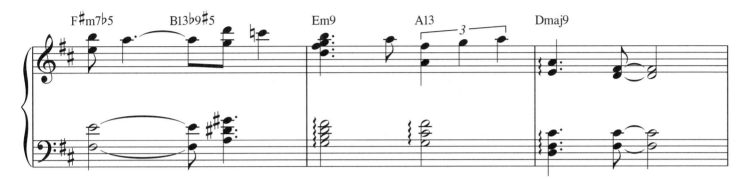

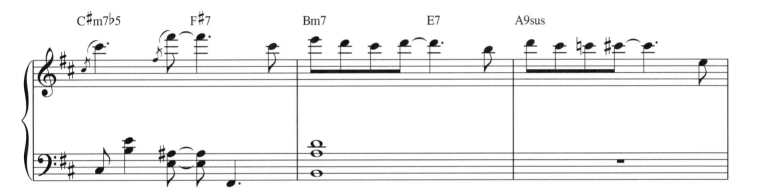

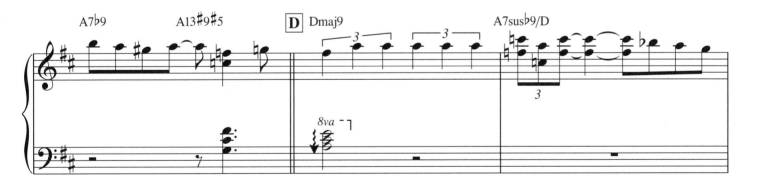

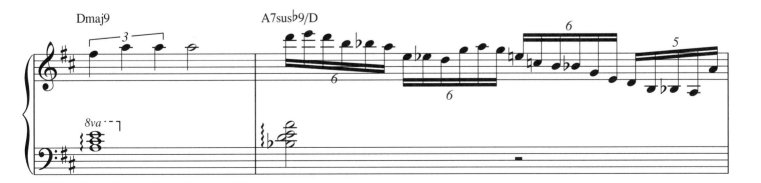

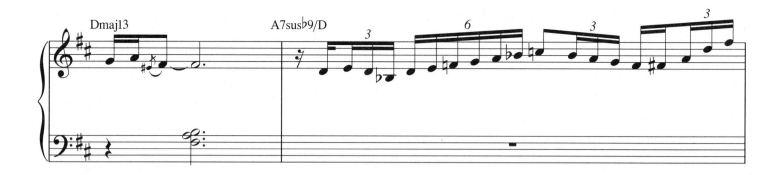

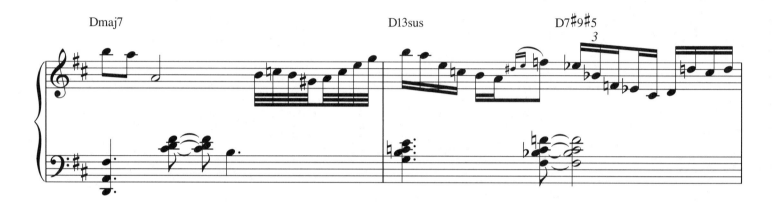

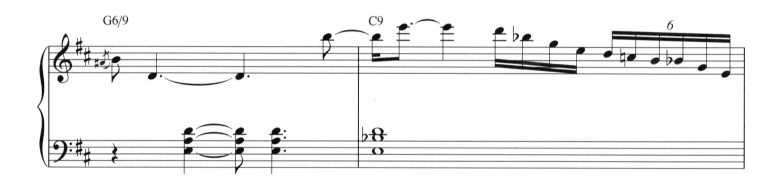

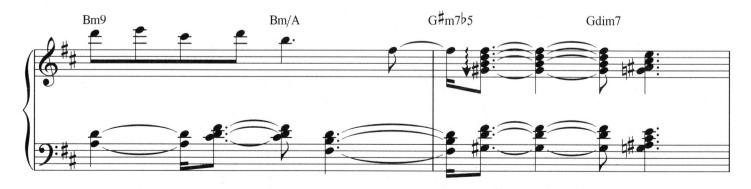

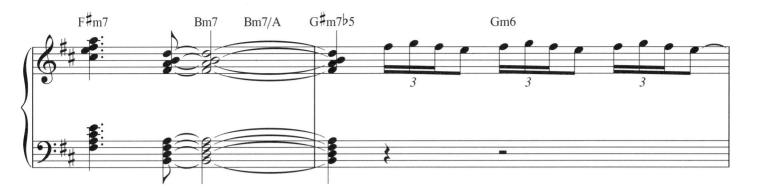

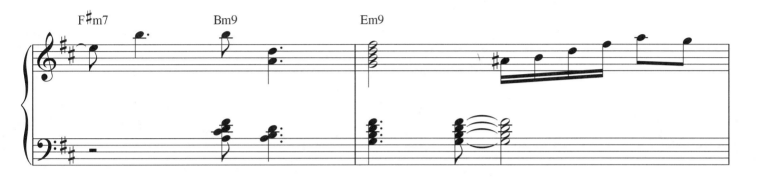

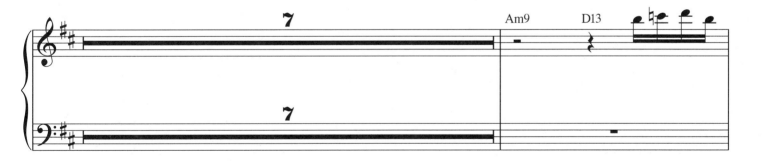

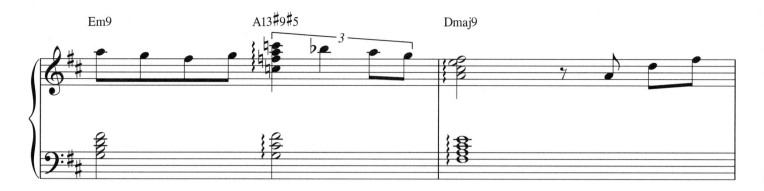

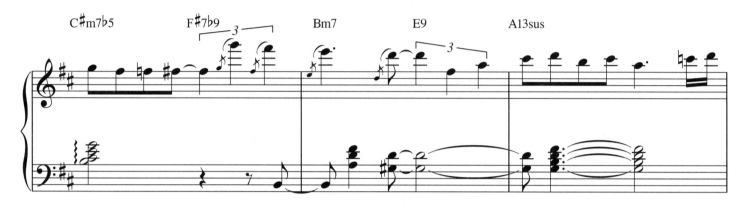

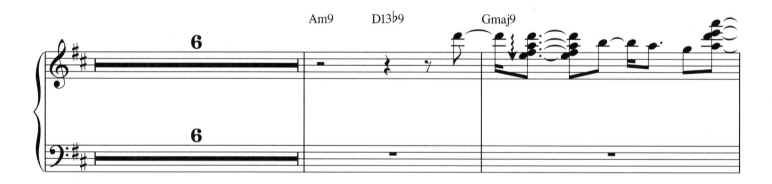

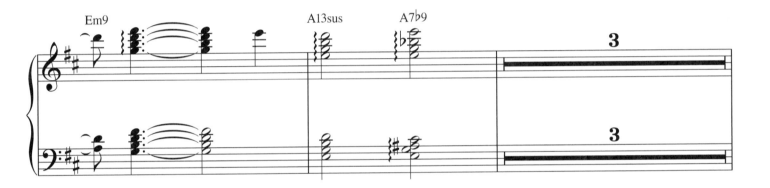

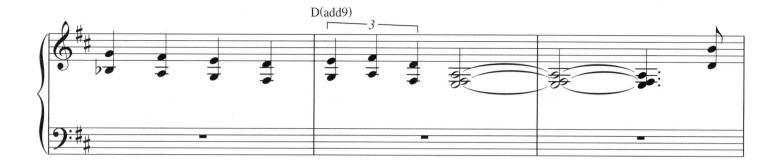

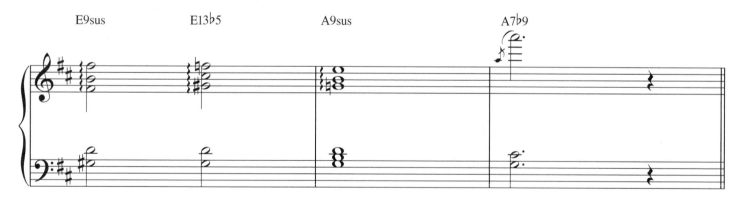

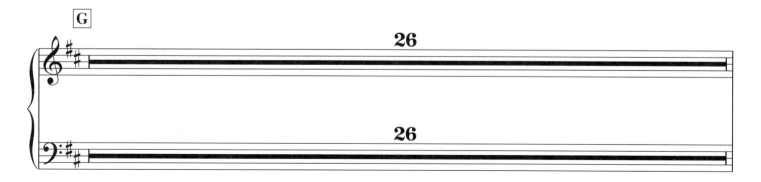

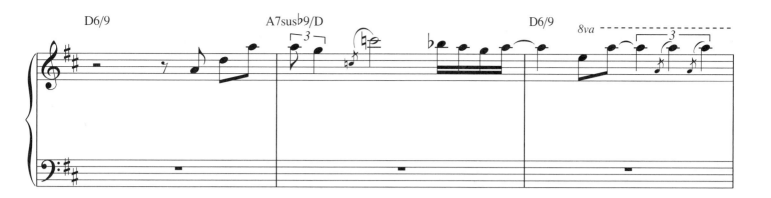

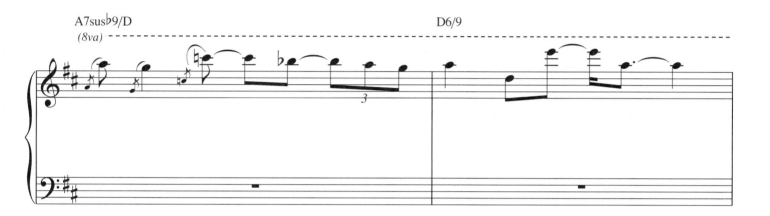

# It's On

## By Oscar Peterson

**Moderate Swing** ♩ = 142

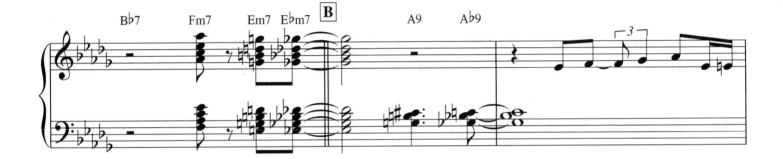

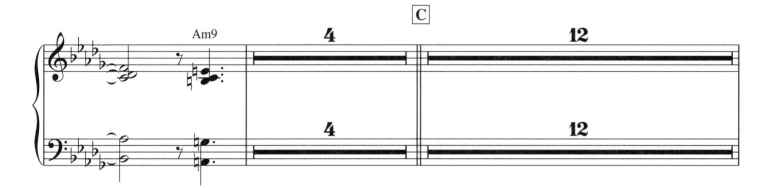

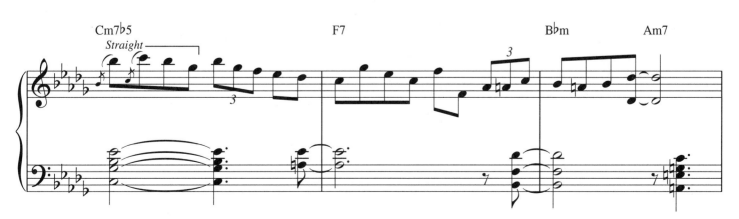

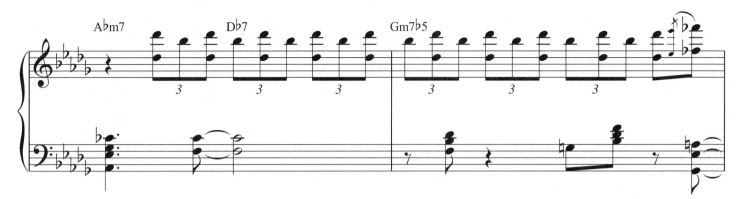

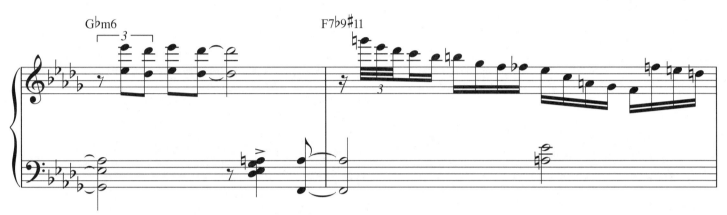

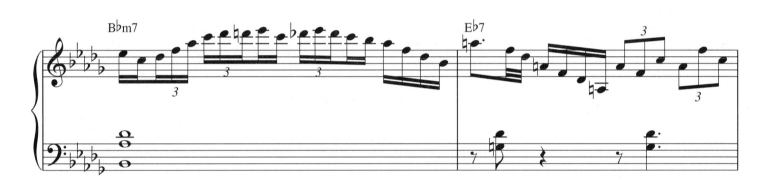

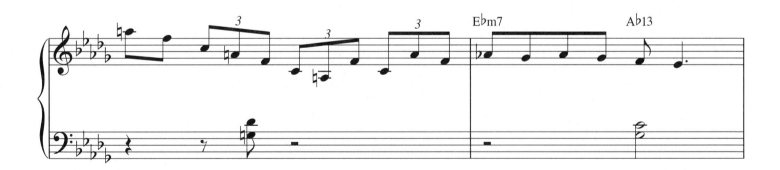

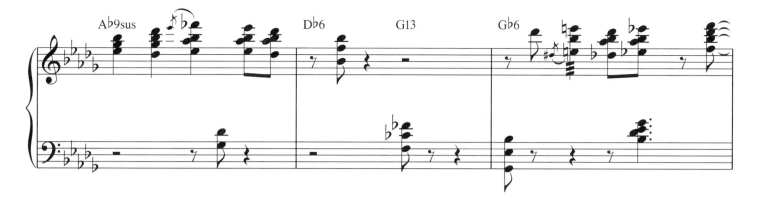

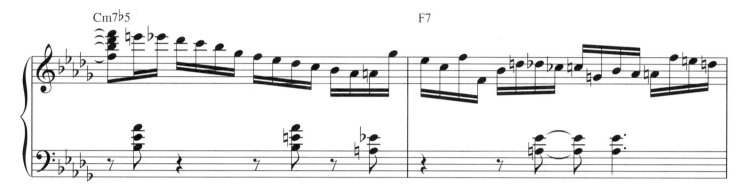

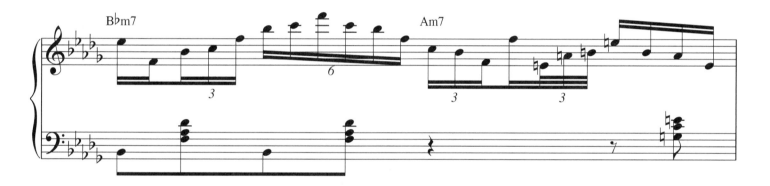

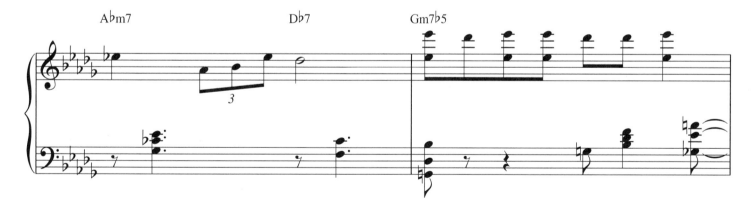

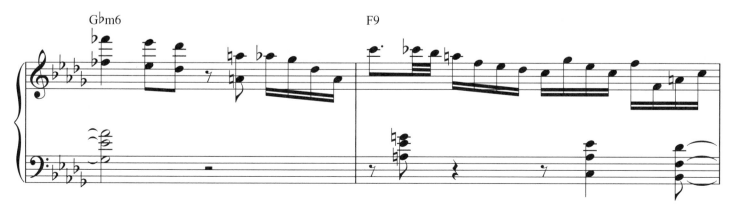

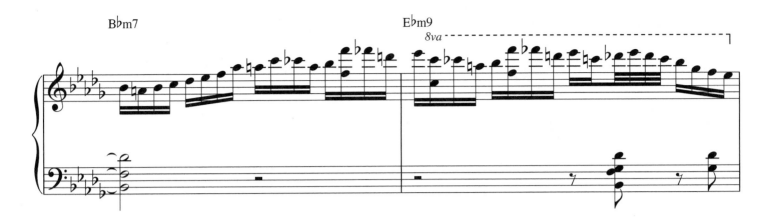

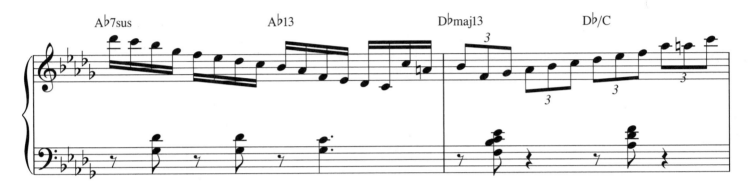

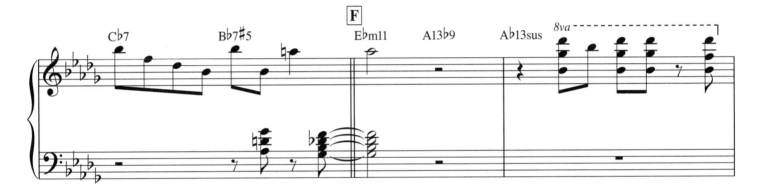

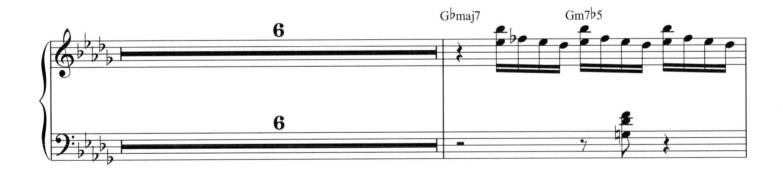

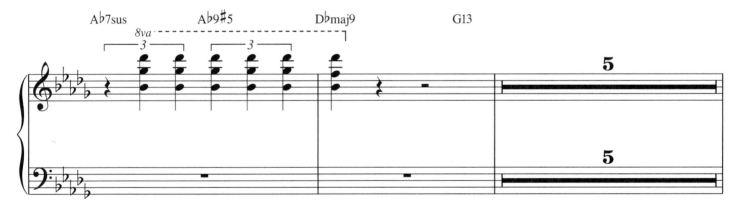

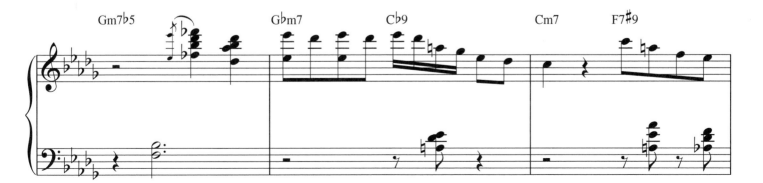

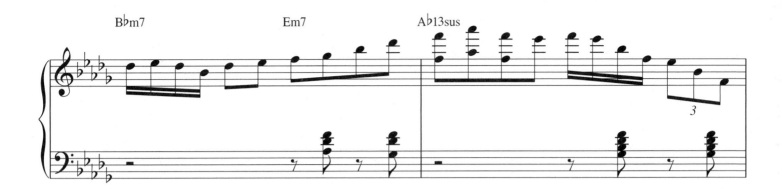

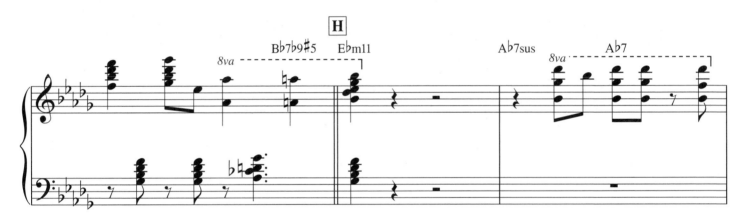

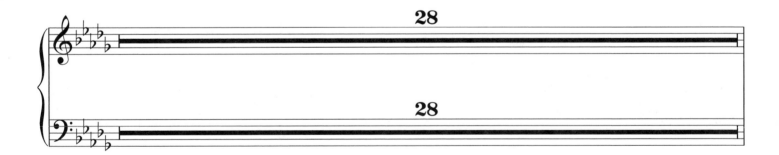

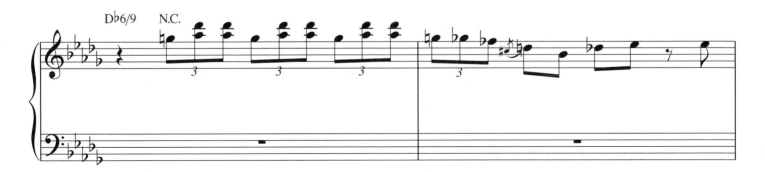

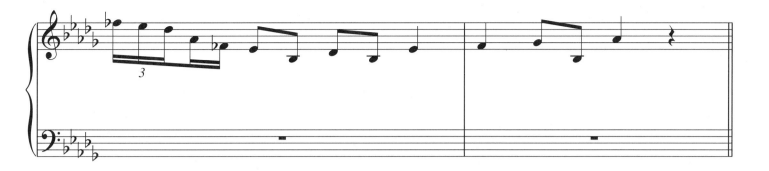

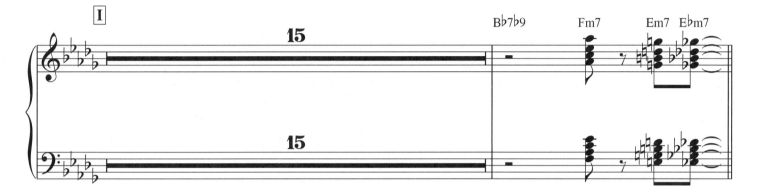

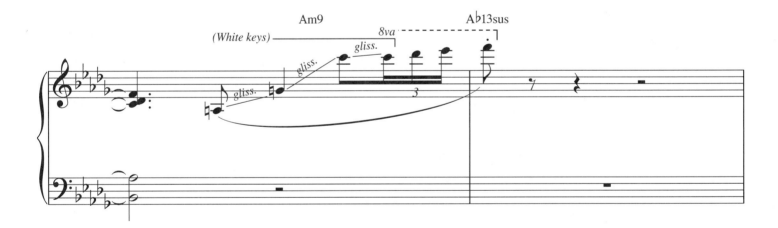

# Heraldry

## By Oscar Peterson

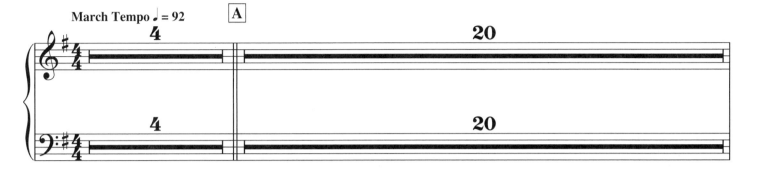

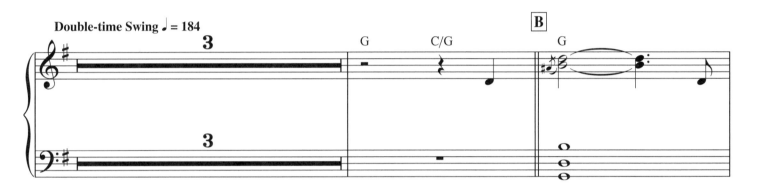

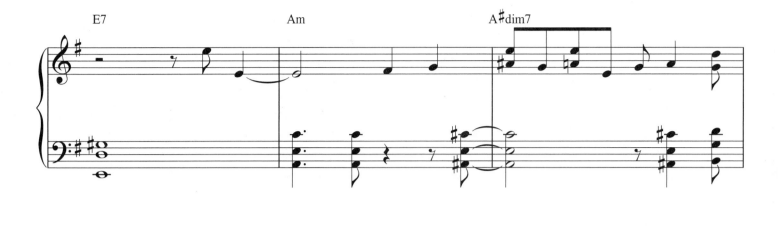

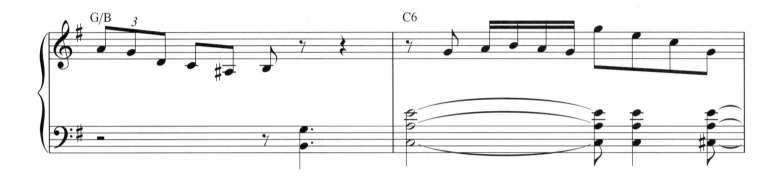

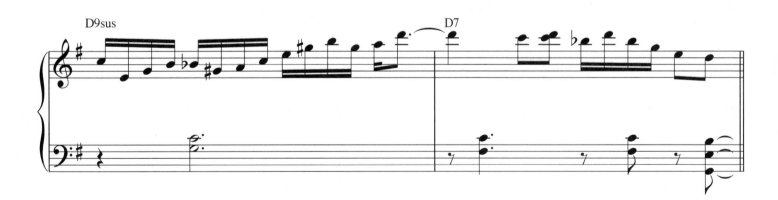

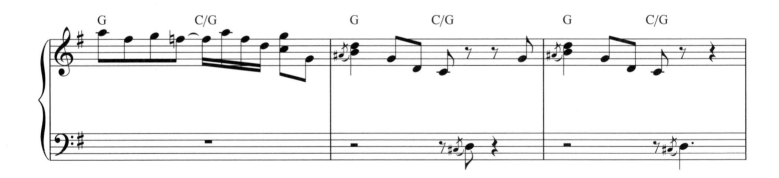

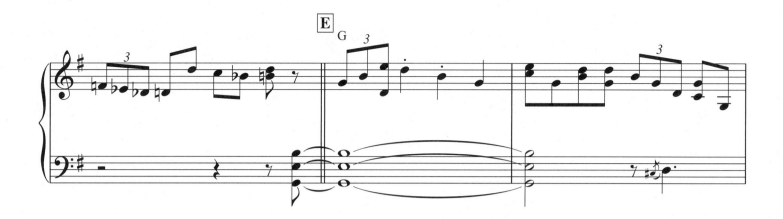

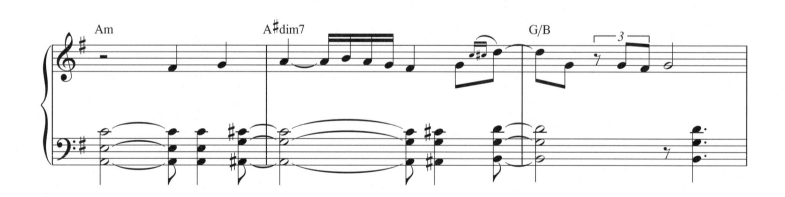

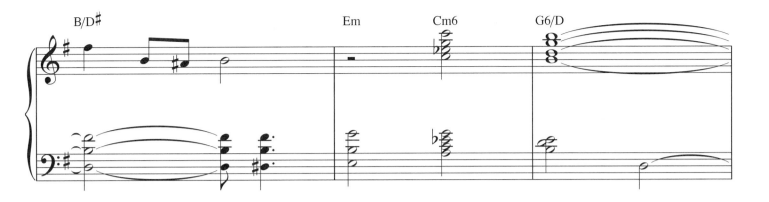

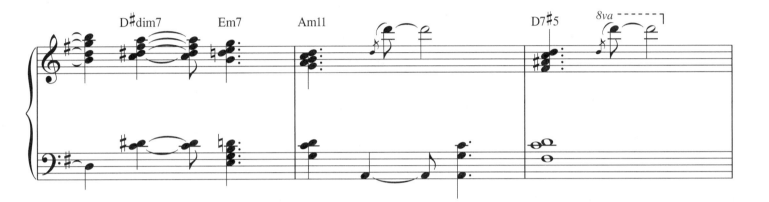

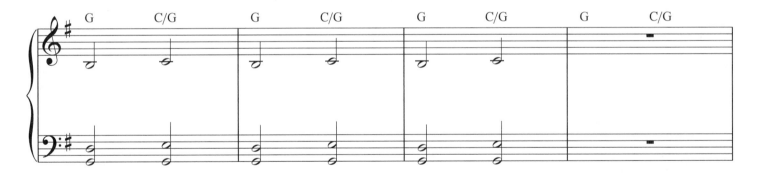

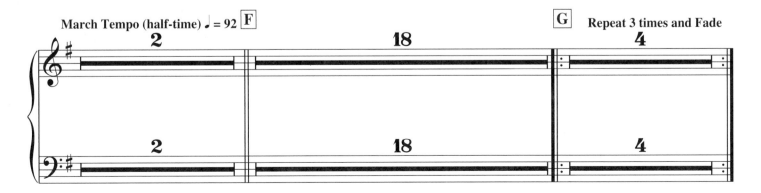

# Royal Honeymoon

## By Oscar Peterson

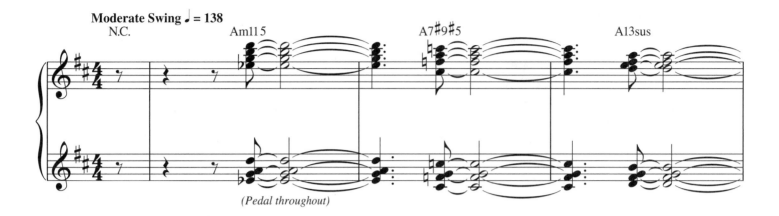

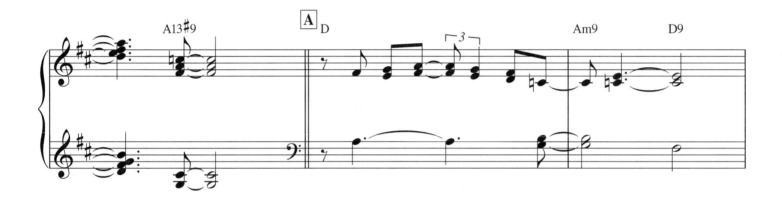

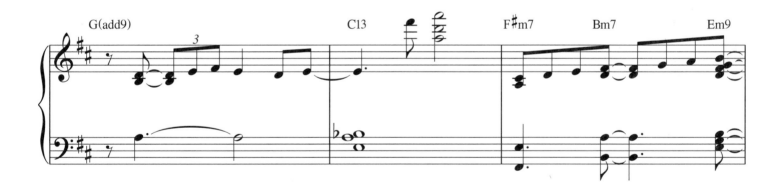

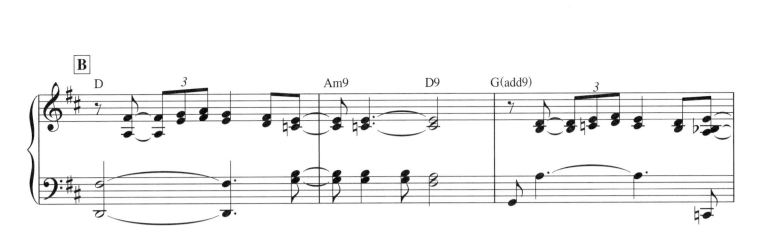

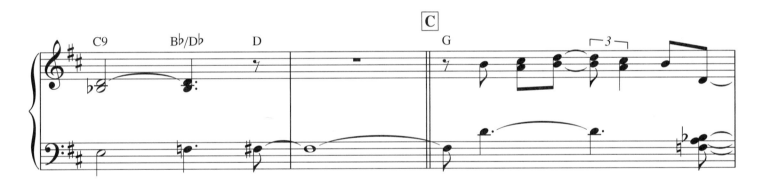

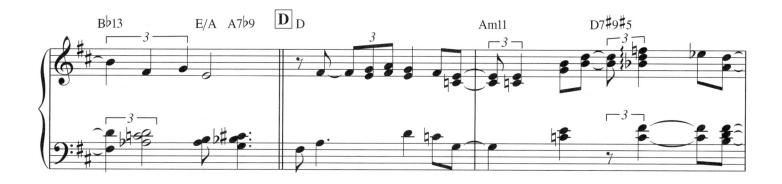

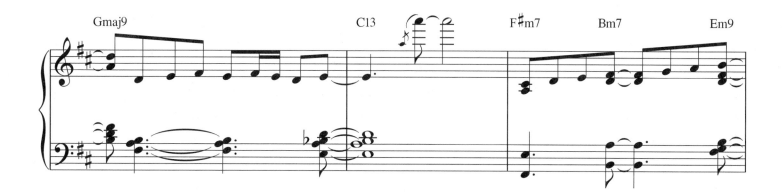

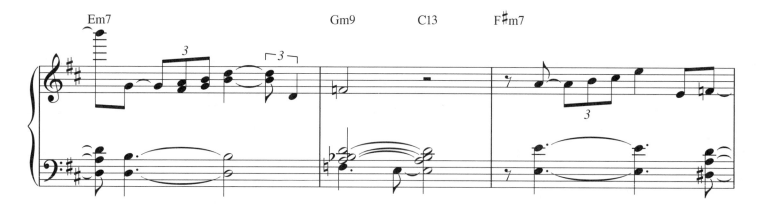

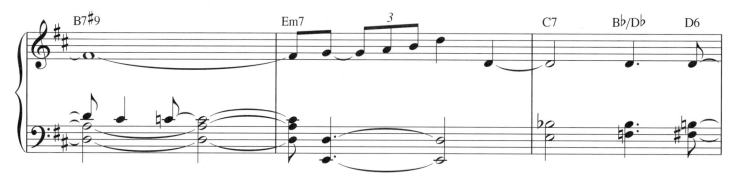

44

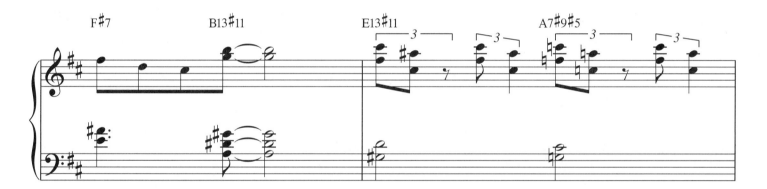

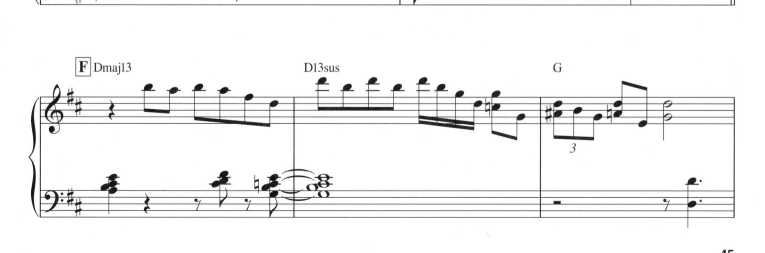

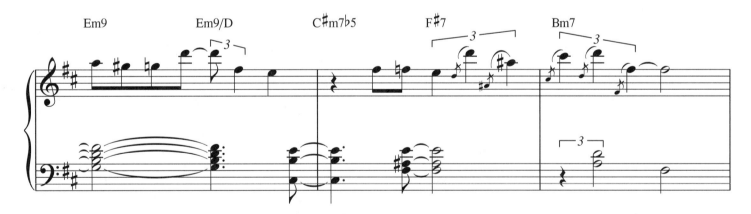

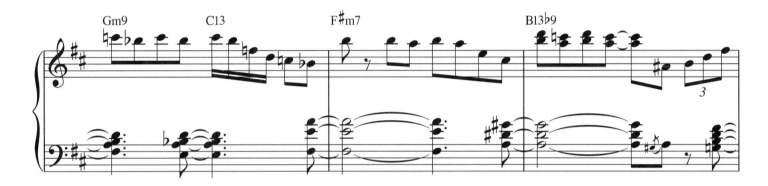

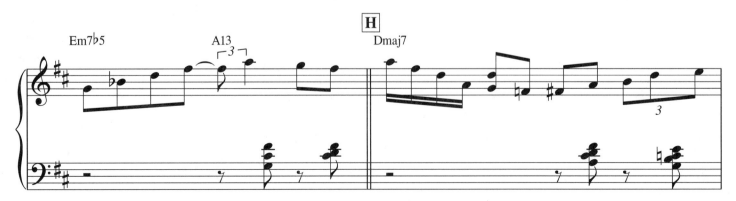

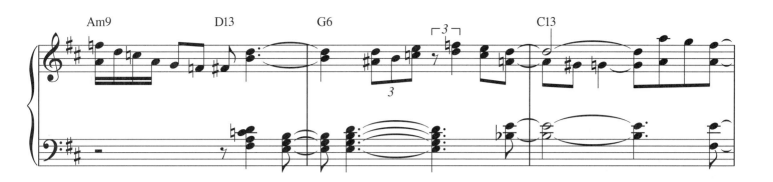

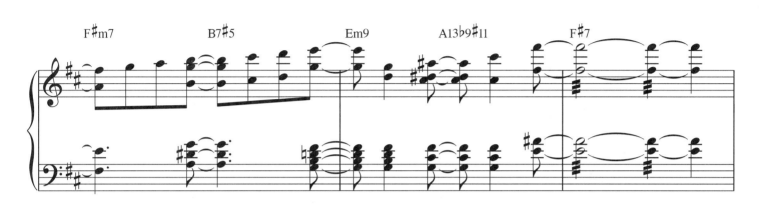

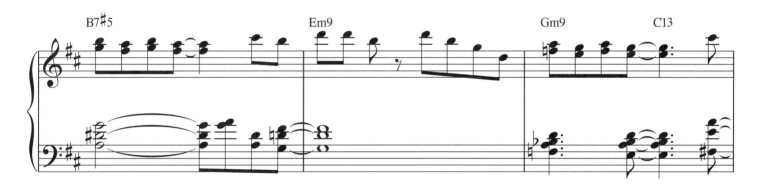

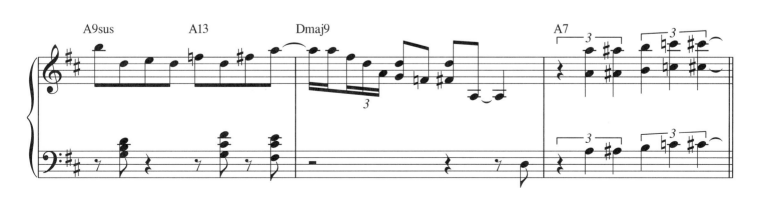

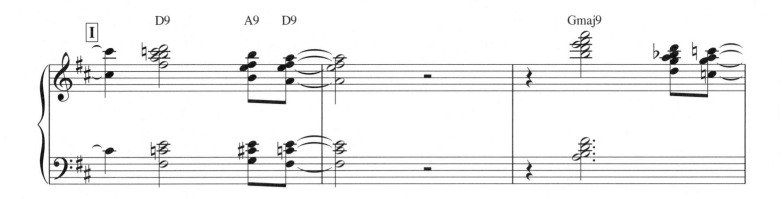

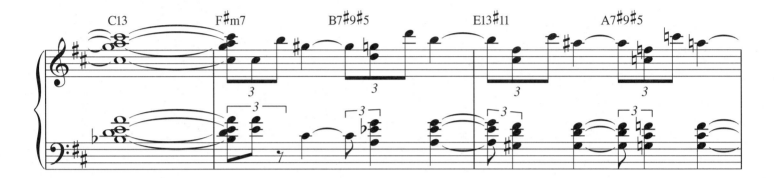

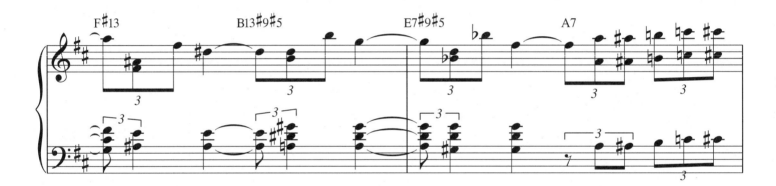

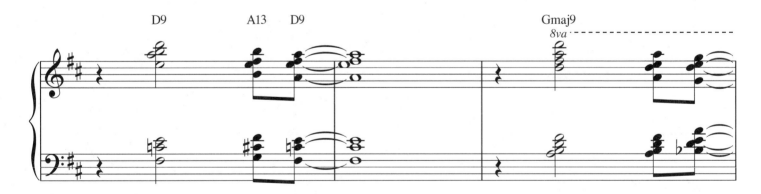

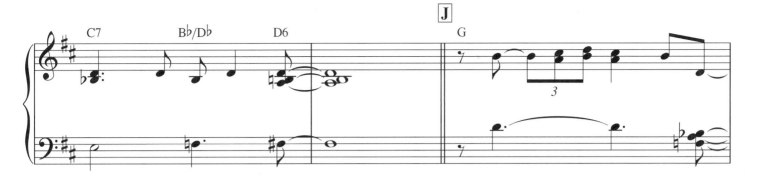

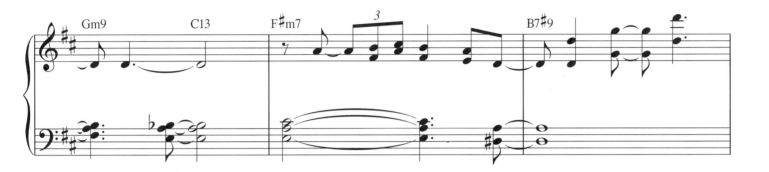

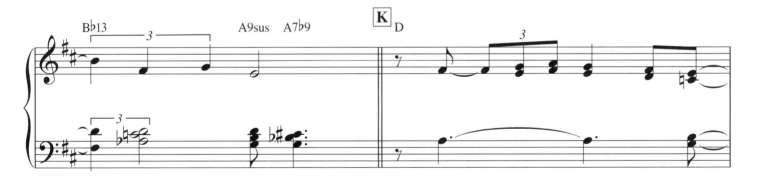

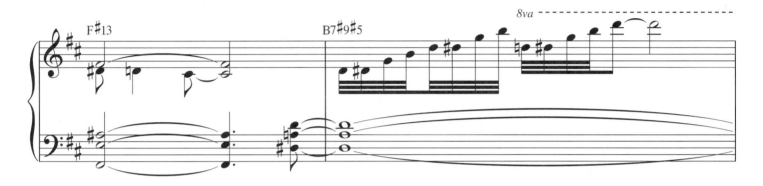

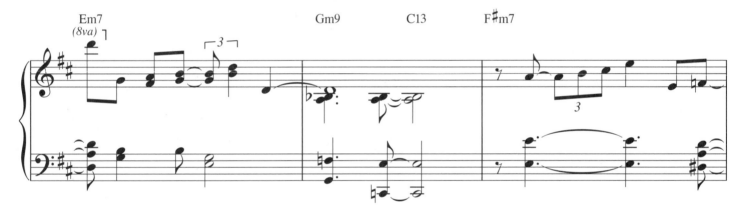

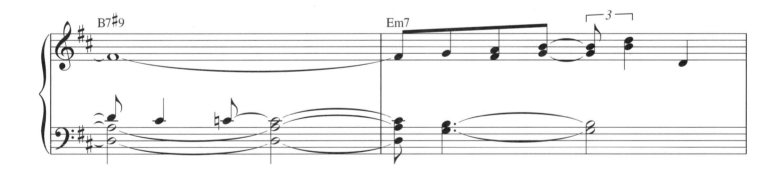

# Jubilation

**By Oscar Peterson**

**Bright Swing** ♩ = 236

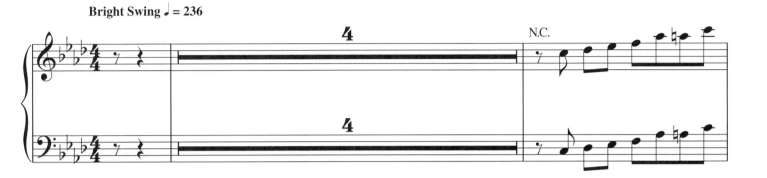

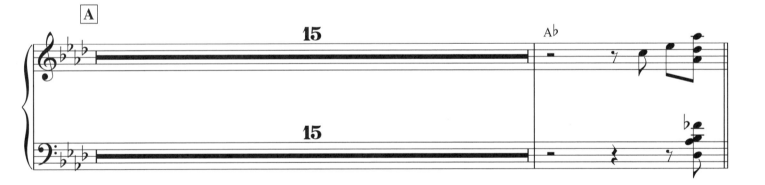

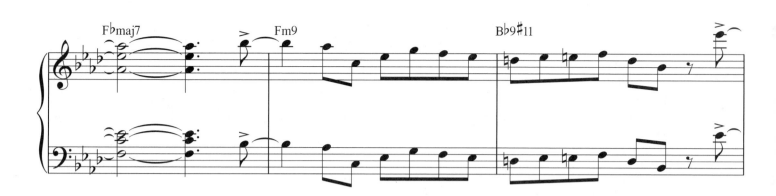

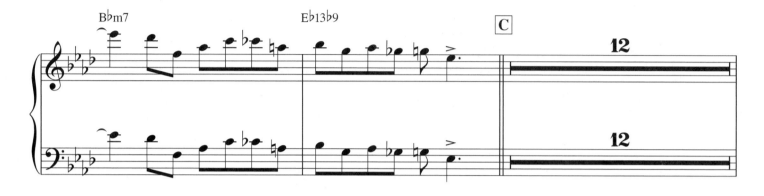

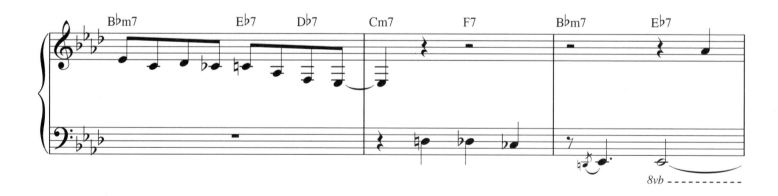

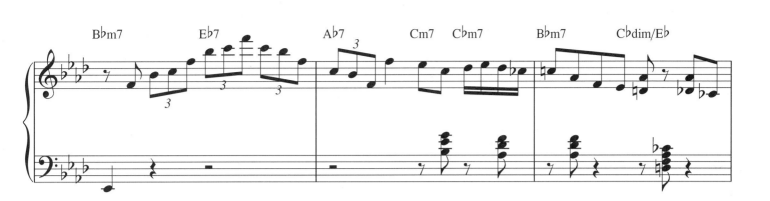

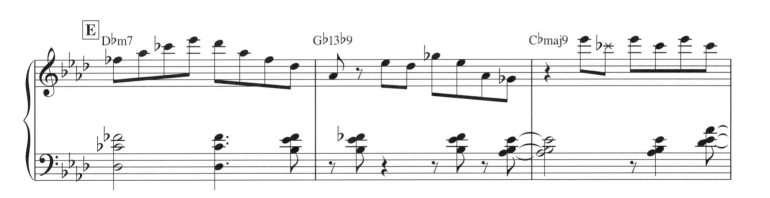

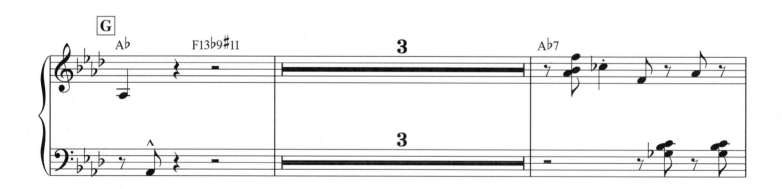

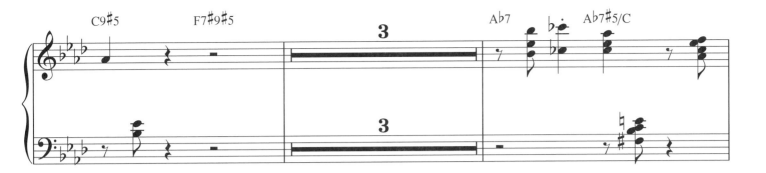

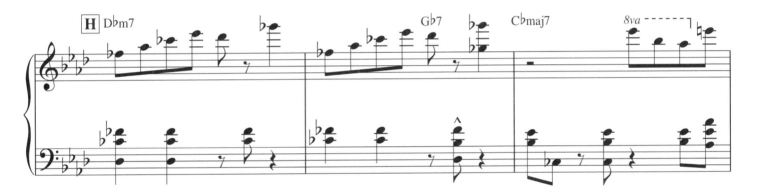

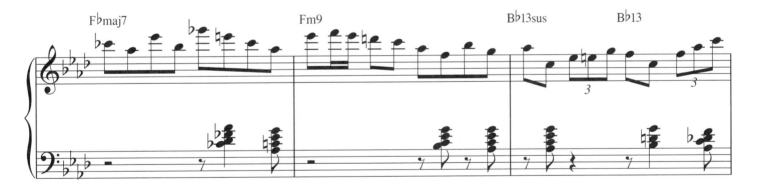

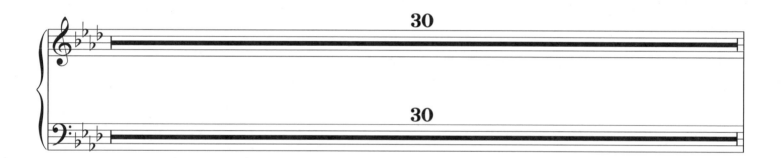

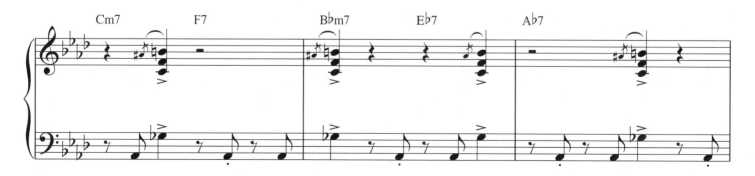

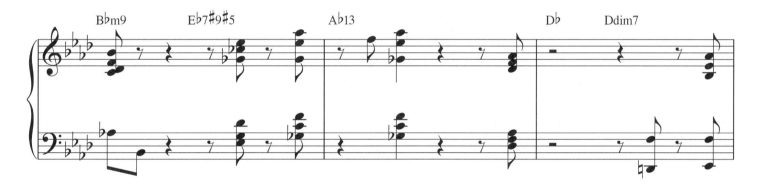

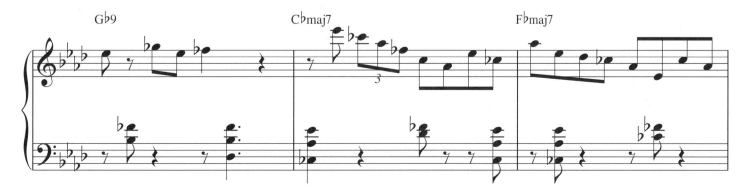

**M** Guitar solo (comping)

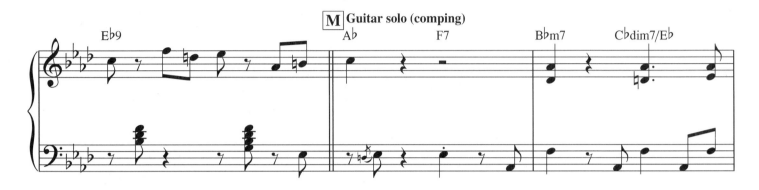

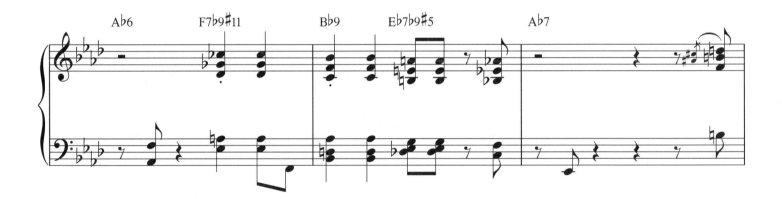

**N**

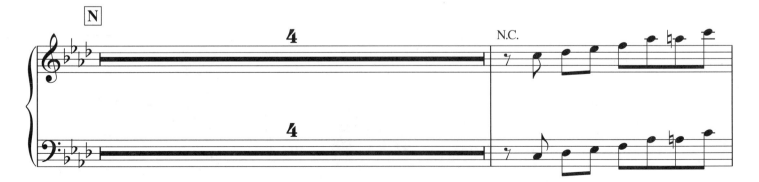

**O**

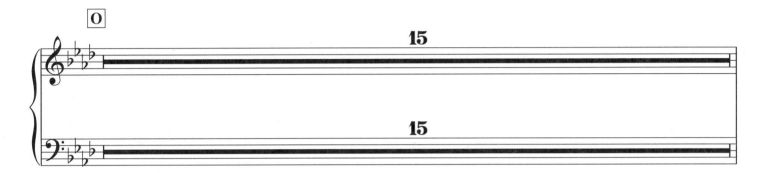

**P**

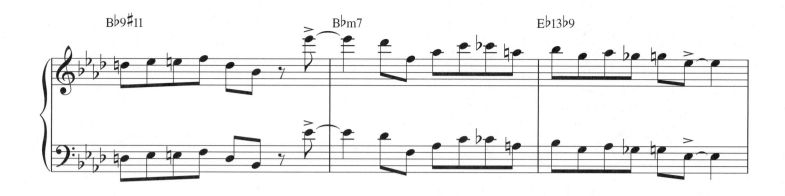

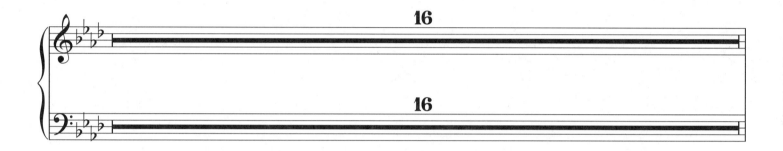

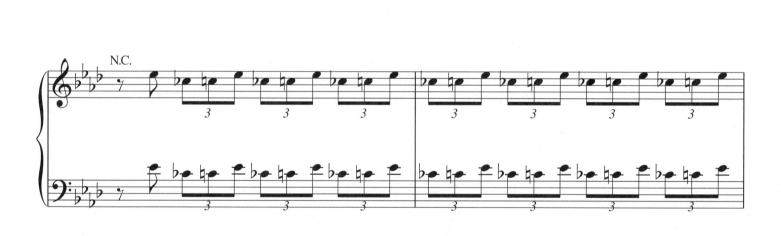

# Lady Di's Waltz

**By Oscar Peterson**

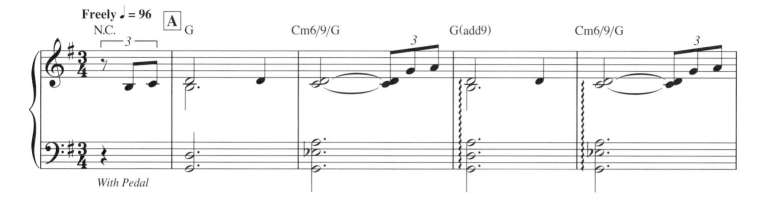

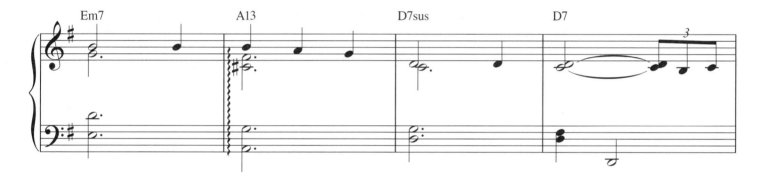

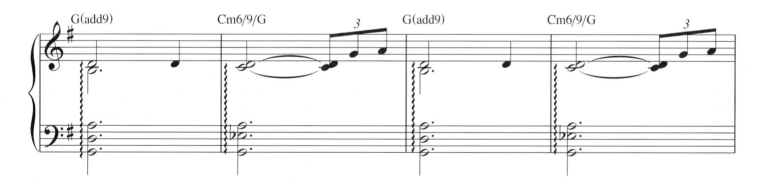

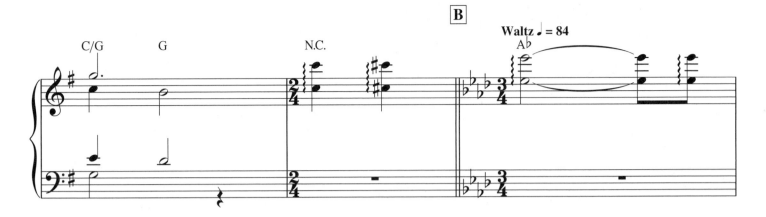

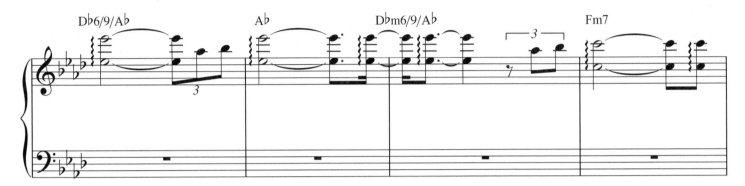

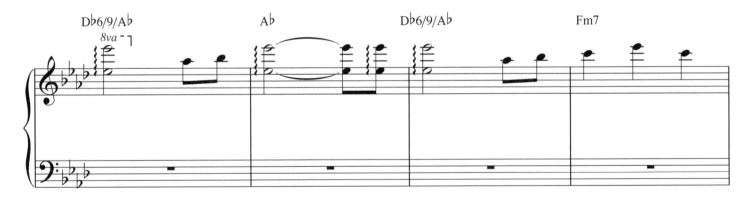

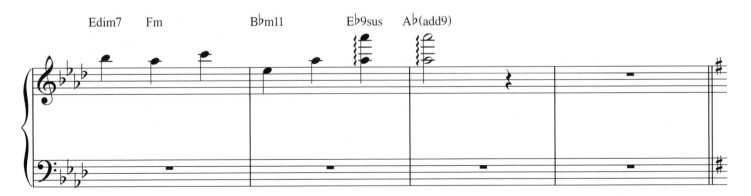

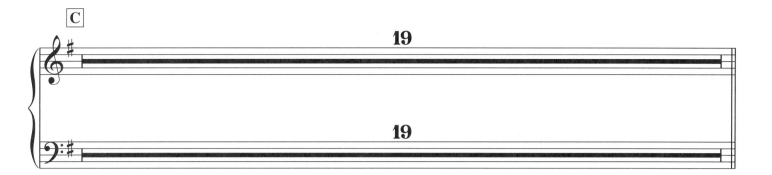

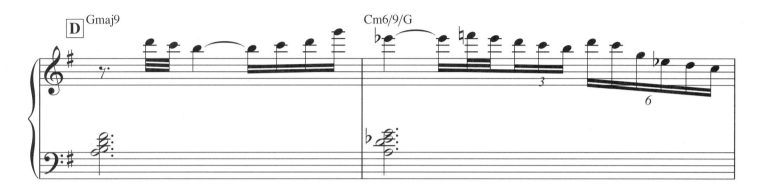

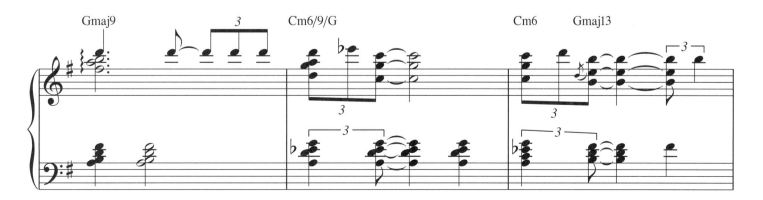

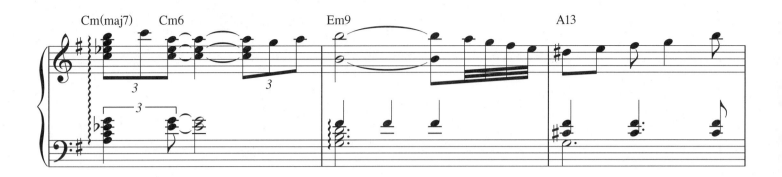

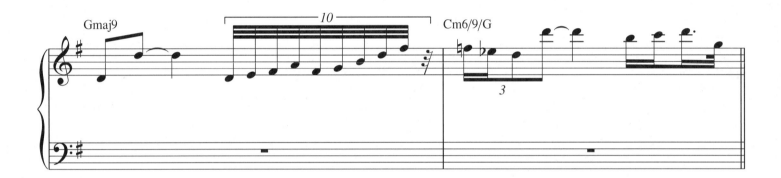

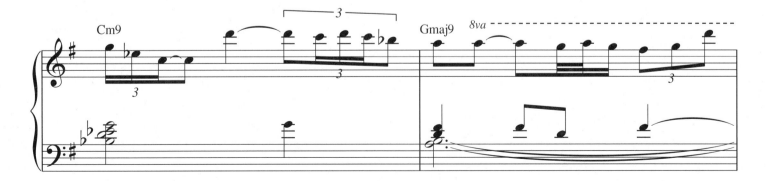

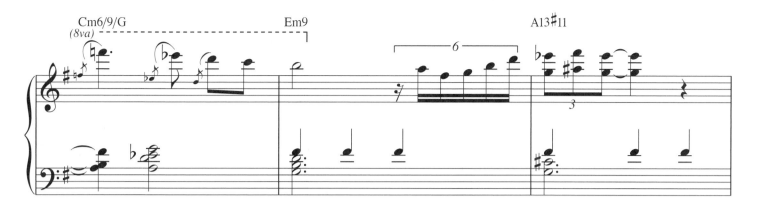

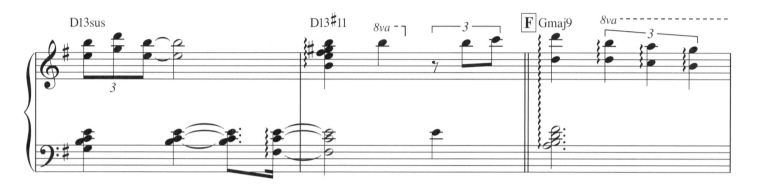

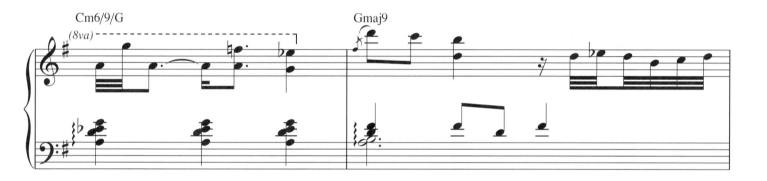

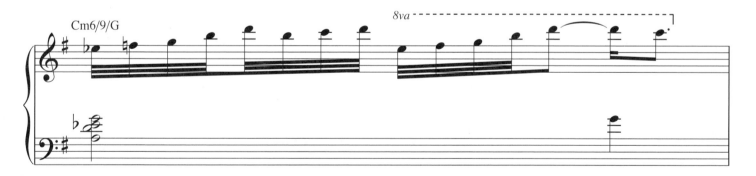

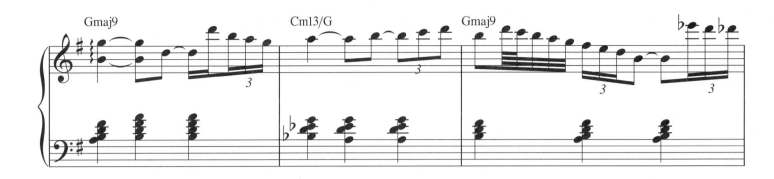

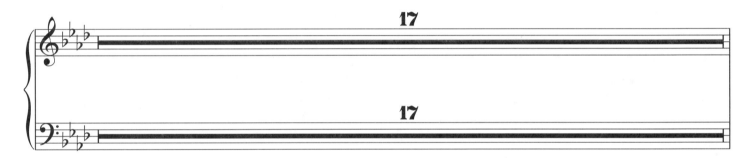

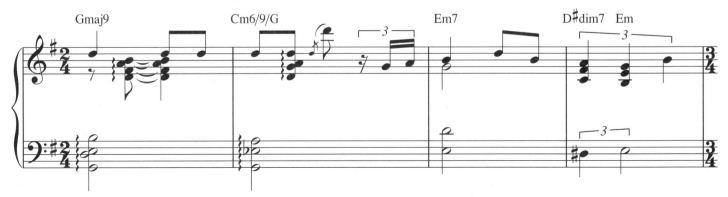

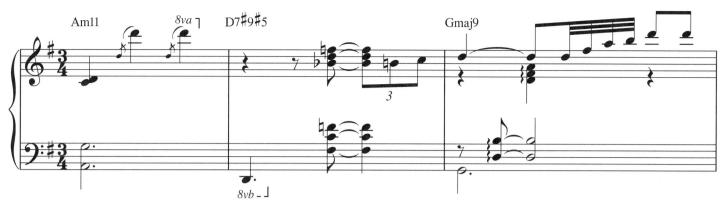

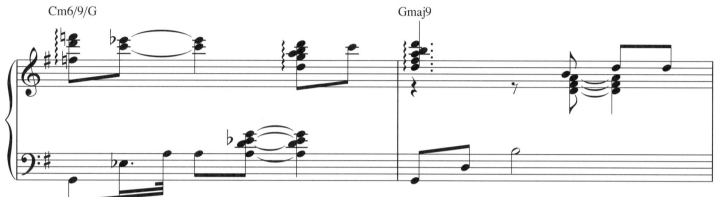

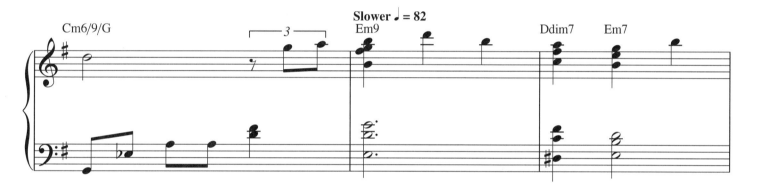

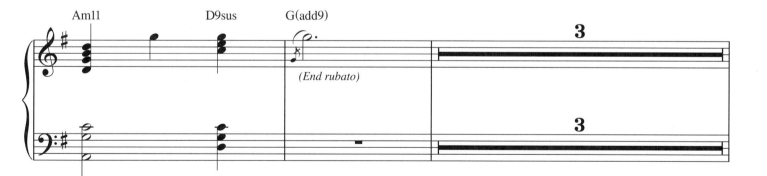

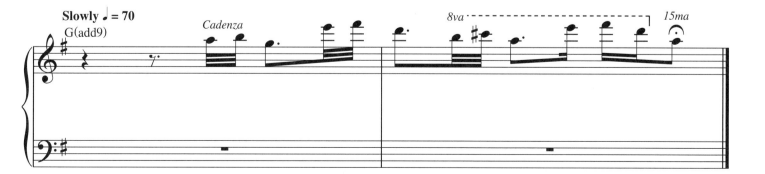

# Let the World Sing

## By Oscar Peterson

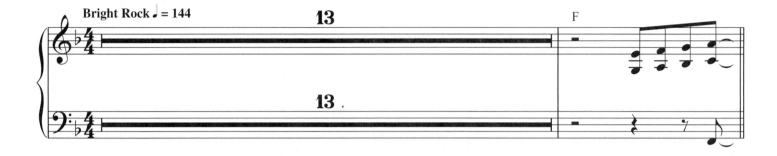

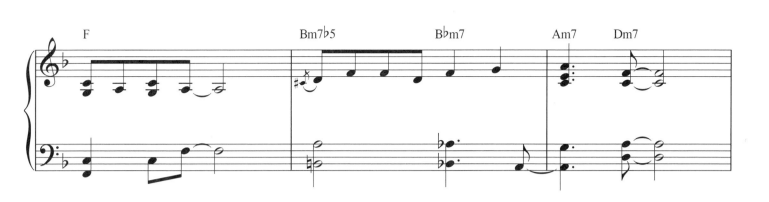

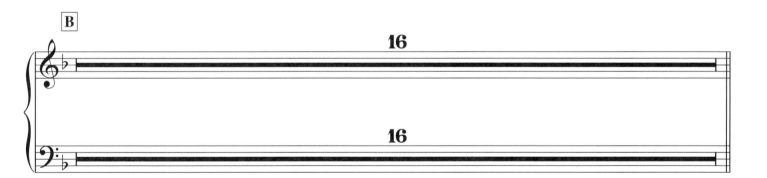

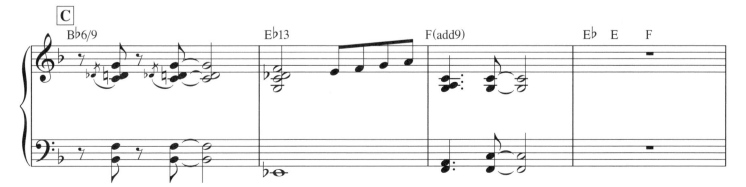

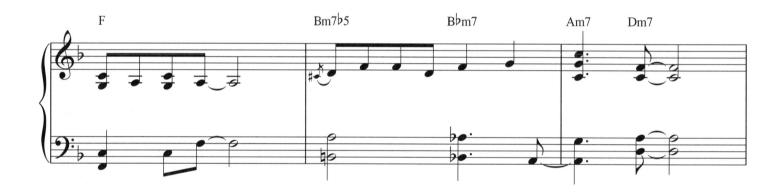

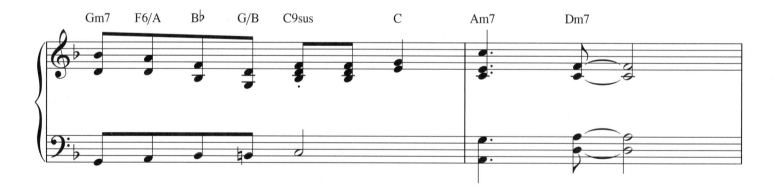

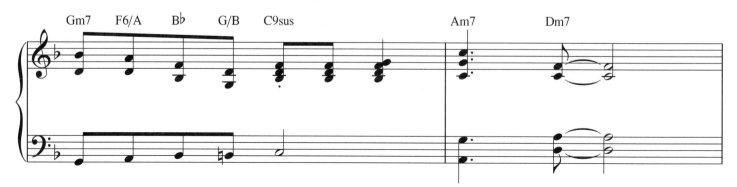

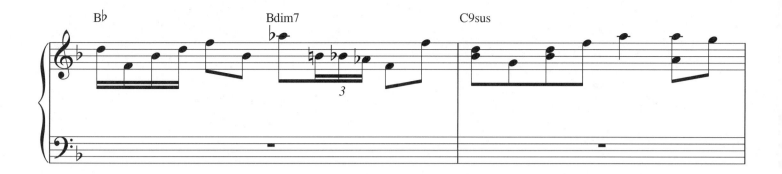

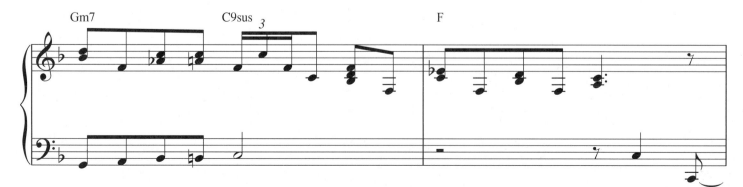

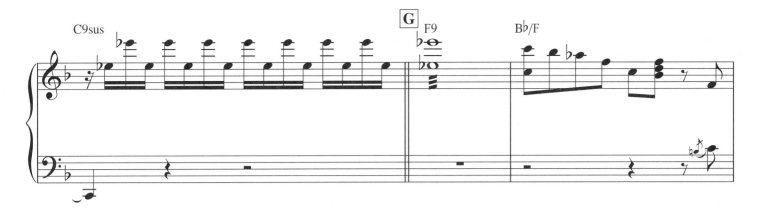

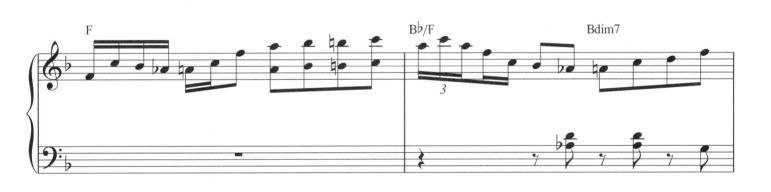

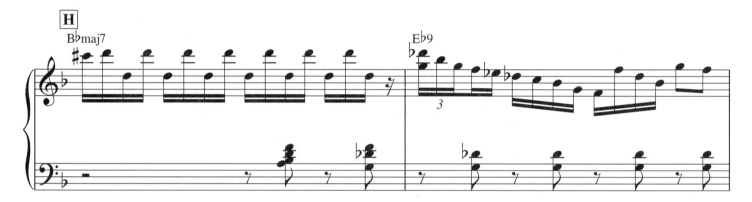

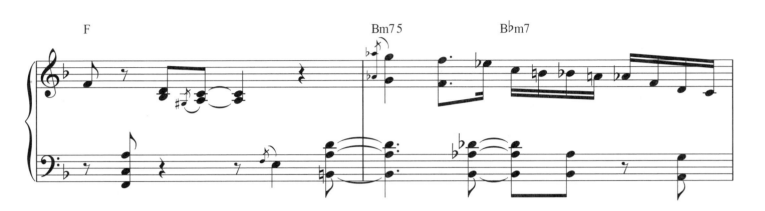

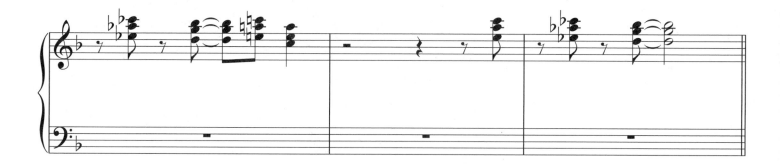

J Guitar solo **31**

**31**

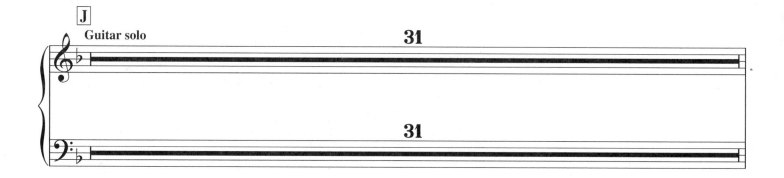

F  K B♭7  E♭7

F  E♭ E F  E♭9

Gm7  C9sus  Am7  Dm7  Gm7  C9sus

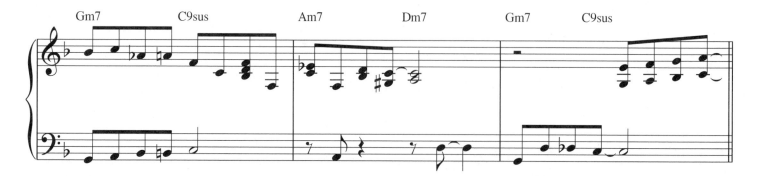

**Bright Rock (Same Tempo)**

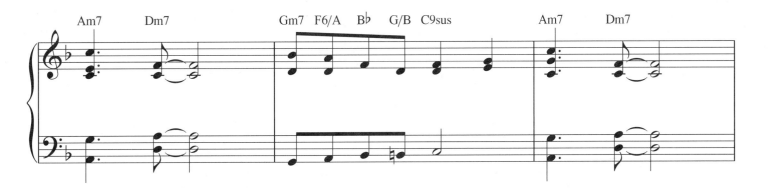

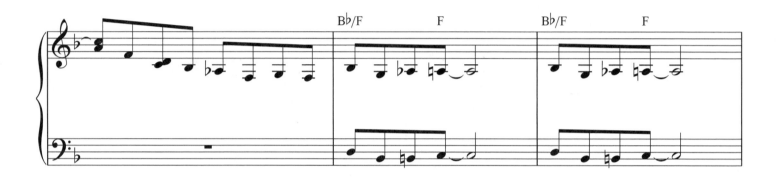

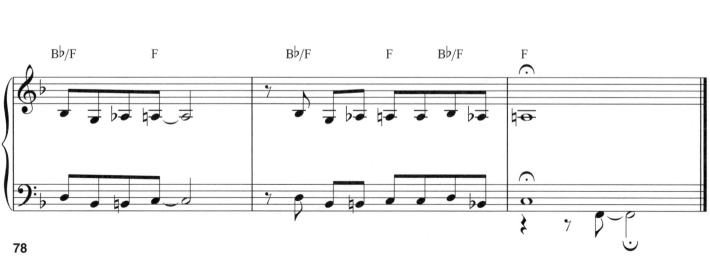

 Presenting the Hal Leonard **JAZZ PLAY-ALONG SERIES**

**1. DUKE ELLINGTON**
00841644 .......................$16.95

**2. MILES DAVIS**
00841645 .......................$16.95

**3. THE BLUES**
00841646 .......................$16.99

**4. JAZZ BALLADS**
00841691 .......................$16.99

**5. BEST OF BEBOP**
00841689 .......................$16.99

**6. JAZZ CLASSICS WITH EASY CHANGES**
00841690 .......................$16.99

**7. ESSENTIAL JAZZ STANDARDS**
00843000 .......................$16.99

**8. ANTONIO CARLOS JOBIM AND THE ART OF THE BOSSA NOVA**
00843001 .......................$16.95

**9. DIZZY GILLESPIE**
00843002 .......................$16.99

**10. DISNEY CLASSICS**
00843003 .......................$16.99

**11. RODGERS AND HART – FAVORITES**
00843004 .......................$16.99

**12. ESSENTIAL JAZZ CLASSICS**
00843005 .......................$16.99

**13. JOHN COLTRANE**
00843006 .......................$16.95

**14. IRVING BERLIN**
00843007 .......................$15.99

**15. RODGERS & HAMMERSTEIN**
00843008 .......................$15.99

**16. COLE PORTER**
00843009 .......................$15.95

**17. COUNT BASIE**
00843010 .......................$16.95

**18. HAROLD ARLEN**
00843011 .......................$16.95

**19. COOL JAZZ**
00843012 .......................$15.95

**20. CHRISTMAS CAROLS**
00843080 .......................$14.95

**21. RODGERS AND HART – CLASSICS**
00843014 .......................$14.95

**22. WAYNE SHORTER**
00843015 .......................$16.95

**23. LATIN JAZZ**
00843016 .......................$16.95

**24. EARLY JAZZ STANDARDS**
00843017 .......................$14.95

**25. CHRISTMAS JAZZ**
00843018 .......................$16.95

**26. CHARLIE PARKER**
00843019 .......................$16.95

**27. GREAT JAZZ STANDARDS**
00843020 .......................$15.99

**28. BIG BAND ERA**
00843021 .......................$15.99

**29. LENNON AND McCARTNEY**
00843022 .......................$16.95

**30. BLUES' BEST**
00843023 .......................$15.99

**31. JAZZ IN THREE**
00843024 .......................$15.99

**32. BEST OF SWING**
00843025 .......................$15.99

**33. SONNY ROLLINS**
00843029 .......................$15.95

**34. ALL TIME STANDARDS**
00843030 .......................$15.99

**35. BLUESY JAZZ**
00843031 .......................$15.99

**36. HORACE SILVER**
00843032 .......................$16.99

**37. BILL EVANS**
00843033 .......................$16.95

**38. YULETIDE JAZZ**
00843034 .......................$16.95

**39. "ALL THE THINGS YOU ARE" & MORE JEROME KERN SONGS**
00843035 .......................$15.99

**40. BOSSA NOVA**
00843036 .......................$15.99

**41. CLASSIC DUKE ELLINGTON**
00843037 .......................$16.99

**42. GERRY MULLIGAN – FAVORITES**
00843038 .......................$16.99
**43. GERRY MULLIGAN – CLASSICS**
00843039 .......................$16.95

**44. OLIVER NELSON**
00843040 .......................$16.95

**45. JAZZ AT THE MOVIES**
00843041 .......................$15.99

**46. BROADWAY JAZZ STANDARDS**
00843042 .......................$15.99

**47. CLASSIC JAZZ BALLADS**
00843043 .......................$15.99

**48. BEBOP CLASSICS**
00843044 .......................$16.99

**49. MILES DAVIS – STANDARDS**
00843045 .......................$16.95

**50. GREAT JAZZ CLASSICS**
00843046 .......................$15.99

**51. UP-TEMPO JAZZ**
00843047 .......................$15.99

**52. STEVIE WONDER**
00843048 .......................$15.95

**53. RHYTHM CHANGES**
00843049 .......................$15.99

**54. "MOONLIGHT IN VERMONT" & OTHER GREAT STANDARDS**
00843050 .......................$15.99

**55. BENNY GOLSON**
00843052 .......................$15.95

**56. "GEORGIA ON MY MIND" & OTHER SONGS BY HOAGY CARMICHAEL**
00843056 .......................$15.99

**57. VINCE GUARALDI**
00843057 .......................$16.99

**58. MORE LENNON AND McCARTNEY**
00843059 .......................$15.99

**59. SOUL JAZZ**
00843060 .......................$15.99

**60. DEXTER GORDON**
00843061 .......................$15.95

**61. MONGO SANTAMARIA**
00843062 .......................$15.95

**62. JAZZ-ROCK FUSION**
00843063 .......................$14.95

**63. CLASSICAL JAZZ**
00843064 .......................$14.95

**64. TV TUNES**
00843065 .......................$14.95

**65. SMOOTH JAZZ**
00843066 .......................$16.99

**66. A CHARLIE BROWN CHRISTMAS**
00843067 .......................$16.99

**67. CHICK COREA**
00843068 .......................$15.95

**68. CHARLES MINGUS**
00843069 .......................$16.95

**69. CLASSIC JAZZ**
00843071 .......................$15.99

**70. THE DOORS**
00843072 .......................$14.95

**71. COLE PORTER CLASSICS**
00843073 .......................$14.95

**72. CLASSIC JAZZ BALLADS**
00843074 .......................$15.99

**73. JAZZ/BLUES**
00843075 .......................$14.95

**74. BEST JAZZ CLASSICS**
00843076 .......................$15.99

**75. PAUL DESMOND**
00843077 .......................$14.95

**76. BROADWAY JAZZ BALLADS**
00843078 .......................$15.99

**77. JAZZ ON BROADWAY**
00843079 .......................$15.99

**78. STEELY DAN**
00843070 .......................$15.99

**79. MILES DAVIS – CLASSICS**
00843081 .......................$15.99

**80. JIMI HENDRIX**
00843083 .......................$15.99

**81. FRANK SINATRA – CLASSICS**
00843084 .......................$15.99

**82. FRANK SINATRA – STANDARDS**
00843085 .......................$15.99

**83. ANDREW LLOYD WEBBER**
00843104 .......................$14.95

**84. BOSSA NOVA CLASSICS**
00843105 .......................$14.95

**85. MOTOWN HITS**
00843109 .......................$14.95

**86. BENNY GOODMAN**
00843110 .......................$14.95

**87. DIXIELAND**
00843111 .......................$14.95

**88. DUKE ELLINGTON FAVORITES**
00843112 .......................$14.95

**89. IRVING BE BRLIN FAVORITES**
00843113 .......................$14.95

**90. THELONIOUS MONK CLASSICS**
00841262 .......................$16.99

**91. THELONIOUS MONK FAVORITES**
00841263 .......................$16.99

**93. DISNEY FAVORITES**
00843142 .......................$14.99

**94. RAY**
00843143 .......................$14.95

**95. JAZZ AT THE LOUNGE**
00843144 .......................$14.99

**96. LATIN JAZZ STANDARDS**
00843145 .......................$14.99

**98. DAVE FRISHBERG**
00843149 .......................$14.99

**105. SOULFUL JAZZ**
00843151 .......................$14.99

**106. SLO' JAZZ**
00843117 .......................$14.99

**107. MOTOWN CLASSICS**
00843116 .......................$14.99

The Hal Leonard JAZZ PLAY-ALONG® SERIES is the ultimate learning tool for all jazz musicians. With musician-friendly lead sheets, melody cues and other split track choices on the included CD, these packs make learning to play jazz easier and more fun than ever before. Parts are included for B♭, E♭, C and Bass Clef instruments.

Prices, contents, and availability subject to change without notice.

FOR MORE INFORMATION, SEE YOUR LOCAL MUSIC DEALER, OR WRITE TO:

**HAL•LEONARD® CORPORATION**
7777 W. BLUEMOUND RD. P.O. BOX 13819
MILWAUKEE, WISCONSIN 53213

Visit Hal Leonard online at
**www.halleonard.com**
for complete songlists.

0109

# ARTIST TRANSCRIPTIONS®

Artist Transcriptions are authentic, note-for-note transcriptions of today's hottest artists in jazz, pop and rock. These outstanding, accurate arrangements are in an easy-to-read format which includes all essential lines. Artist Transcriptions can be used to perform, sequence or for reference.

## CLARINET

| | | |
|---|---|---|
| 00672423 | Buddy De Franco Collection | $19.95 |

## FLUTE

| | | |
|---|---|---|
| 00672379 | Eric Dolphy Collection | $19.95 |
| 00672372 | James Moody Collection – Sax and Flute | $19.95 |
| 00660108 | James Newton – Improvising Flute | $14.95 |
| 00672455 | Lew Tabackin Collection | $19.95 |

## GUITAR & BASS

| | | |
|---|---|---|
| 00660113 | The Guitar Style of George Benson | $14.95 |
| 00699072 | Guitar Book of Pierre Bensusan | $29.95 |
| 00672331 | Ron Carter – Acoustic Bass | $16.95 |
| 00672307 | Stanley Clarke Collection | $19.95 |
| 00660115 | Al Di Meola – Friday Night in San Francisco | $14.95 |
| 00604043 | Al Di Meola – Music, Words, Pictures | $14.95 |
| 00673245 | Jazz Style of Tal Farlow | $19.95 |
| 00672359 | Bela Fleck and the Flecktones | $18.95 |
| 00699389 | Jim Hall – Jazz Guitar Environments | $19.95 |
| 00699306 | Jim Hall – Exploring Jazz Guitar | $19.95 |
| 00604049 | Allan Holdsworth – Reaching for the Uncommon Chord | $14.95 |
| 00699215 | Leo Kottke – Eight Songs | $14.95 |
| 00672356 | Jazz Guitar Standards | $19.95 |
| 00675536 | Wes Montgomery – Guitar Transcriptions | $17.95 |
| 00672353 | Joe Pass Collection | $18.95 |
| 00673216 | John Patitucci | $16.95 |
| 00027083 | Django Reinhardt Antholog | $14.95 |
| 00026711 | Genius of Django Reinhardt | $10.95 |
| 00026715 | Django Reinhardt - A Treasury of Songs | $12.95 |
| 00672374 | Johnny Smith Guitar Solos | $16.95 |
| 00672320 | Mark Whitfield | $19.95 |

## PIANO & KEYBOARD

| | | |
|---|---|---|
| 00672338 | Monty Alexander Collection | $19.95 |
| 00672487 | Monty Alexander Plays Standards | $19.95 |
| 00672318 | Kenny Barron Collection | $22.95 |
| 00672520 | Count Basie Collection | $19.95 |
| 00672364 | Warren Bernhardt Collection | $19.95 |
| 00672439 | Cyrus Chestnut Collection | $19.95 |
| 00673242 | Billy Childs Collection | $19.95 |
| 00672300 | Chick Corea – Paint the World | $12.95 |
| 00672537 | Bill Evans at Town Hall | $16.95 |
| 00672425 | Bill Evans – Piano Interpretations | $19.95 |
| 00672365 | Bill Evans – Piano Standards | $19.95 |
| 00672510 | Bill Evans Trio – Vol. 1: 1959-1961 | $24.95 |
| 00672511 | Bill Evans Trio – Vol. 2: 1962-1965 | $24.95 |
| 00672512 | Bill Evans Trio – Vol. 3: 1968-1974 | $24.95 |
| 00672513 | Bill Evans Trio – Vol. 4: 1979-1980 | $24.95 |
| 00672381 | Tommy Flanagan Collection | $19.95 |
| 00672492 | Benny Goodman Collection | $16.95 |
| 00672329 | Benny Green Collection | $19.95 |

| | | |
|---|---|---|
| 00672486 | Vince Guaraldi Collection | $19.95 |
| 00672419 | Herbie Hancock Collection | $19.95 |
| 00672438 | Hampton Hawes | $19.95 |
| 00672322 | Ahmad Jamal Collection | $22.95 |
| 00672476 | Brad Mehldau Collection | $19.95 |
| 00672388 | Best of Thelonious Monk | $19.95 |
| 00672389 | Thelonious Monk Collection | $19.95 |
| 00672390 | Thelonious Monk Plays Jazz Standards – Volume 1 | $19.95 |
| 00672391 | Thelonious Monk Plays Jazz Standards – Volume 2 | $19.95 |
| 00672433 | Jelly Roll Morton – The Piano Rolls | $12.95 |
| 00672553 | Charlie Parker for Piano | $19.95 |
| 00672542 | Oscar Peterson – Jazz Piano Solos | $16.95 |
| 00672544 | Oscar Peterson – Originals | $9.95 |
| 00672532 | Oscar Peterson – Plays Broadway | $19.95 |
| 00672531 | Oscar Peterson – Plays Duke Ellington | $19.95 |
| 00672533 | Oscar Peterson – Trios | $24.95 |
| 00672543 | Oscar Peterson Trio – Canadiana Suite | $9.95 |
| 00672534 | Very Best of Oscar Peterson | $22.95 |
| 00672371 | Bud Powell Classics | $19.95 |
| 00672376 | Bud Powell Collection | $19.95 |
| 00672437 | André Previn Collection | $19.95 |
| 00672507 | Gonzalo Rubalcaba Collection | $19.95 |
| 00672303 | Horace Silver Collection | $19.95 |
| 00672316 | Art Tatum Collection | $22.95 |
| 00672355 | Art Tatum Solo Book | $19.95 |
| 00672357 | Billy Taylor Collection | $24.95 |
| 00673215 | McCoy Tyner | $16.95 |
| 00672321 | Cedar Walton Collection | $19.95 |
| 00672519 | Kenny Werner Collection | $19.95 |
| 00672434 | Teddy Wilson Collection | $19.95 |

## SAXOPHONE

| | | |
|---|---|---|
| 00673244 | Julian "Cannonball" Adderley Collection | $19.95 |
| 00673237 | Michael Brecker | $19.95 |
| 00672429 | Michael Brecker Collection | $19.95 |
| 00672447 | Best of the Brecker Brothers | $19.95 |
| 00672315 | Benny Carter Plays Standards | $22.95 |
| 00672314 | Benny Carter Collection | $22.95 |
| 00672394 | James Carter Collection | $19.95 |
| 00672349 | John Coltrane Plays Giant Steps | $19.95 |
| 00672529 | John Coltrane – Giant Steps | $14.95 |
| 00672494 | John Coltrane – A Love Supreme | $14.95 |
| 00672493 | John Coltrane Plays "Coltrane Changes" | $19.95 |
| 00672453 | John Coltrane Plays Standards | $19.95 |
| 00673233 | John Coltrane Solos | $22.95 |
| 00672328 | Paul Desmond Collection | $19.95 |
| 00672379 | Eric Dolphy Collection | $19.95 |
| 00672530 | Kenny Garrett Collection | $19.95 |
| 00699375 | Stan Getz | $19.95 |
| 00672377 | Stan Getz – Bossa Novas | $19.95 |
| 00672375 | Stan Getz – Standards | $18.95 |
| 00673254 | Great Tenor Sax Solos | $18.95 |
| 00672523 | Coleman Hawkins Collection | $19.95 |

| | | |
|---|---|---|
| 00673252 | Joe Henderson – Selections from "Lush Life" & "So Near So Far" | $19.95 |
| 00672330 | Best of Joe Henderson | $22.95 |
| 00673239 | Best of Kenny G | $19.95 |
| 00673229 | Kenny G – Breathless | $19.95 |
| 00672462 | Kenny G – Classics in the Key of G | $19.95 |
| 00672485 | Kenny G – Faith: A Holiday Album | $14.95 |
| 00672373 | Kenny G – The Moment | $19.95 |
| 00672326 | Joe Lovano Collection | $19.95 |
| 00672498 | Jackie McLean Collection | $19.95 |
| 00672372 | James Moody Collection – Sax and Flute | $19.95 |
| 00672416 | Frank Morgan Collection | $19.95 |
| 00672539 | Gerry Mulligan Collection | $19.95 |
| 00672352 | Charlie Parker Collection | $19.95 |
| 00672561 | Best of Sonny Rollins | $19.95 |
| 00672444 | Sonny Rollins Collection | $19.95 |
| 00675000 | David Sanborn Collection | $17.95 |
| 00672528 | Bud Shank Collection | $19.95 |
| 00672491 | New Best of Wayne Shorter | $19.95 |
| 00672455 | Lew Tabackin Collection | $19.95 |
| 00672350 | Tenor Saxophone Standards | $18.95 |
| 00672334 | Stanley Turrentine Collection | $19.95 |
| 00672524 | Lester Young Collection | $19.95 |

## TROMBONE

| | | |
|---|---|---|
| 00672332 | J.J. Johnson Collection | $19.95 |
| 00672489 | Steve Turré Collection | $19.95 |

## TRUMPET

| | | |
|---|---|---|
| 00672557 | Herb Alpert Collection | $14.95 |
| 00672480 | Louis Armstrong Collection | $17.95 |
| 00672481 | Louis Armstrong Plays Standards | $17.95 |
| 00672435 | Chet Baker Collection | $19.95 |
| 00672556 | Best of Chris Botti | $19.95 |
| 00673234 | Randy Brecker | $17.95 |
| 00672447 | Best of the Brecker Brothers | $19.95 |
| 00672448 | Miles Davis – Originals, Vol. 1 | $19.95 |
| 00672451 | Miles Davis – Originals, Vol. 2 | $19.95 |
| 00672450 | Miles Davis – Standards, Vol. 1 | $19.95 |
| 00672449 | Miles Davis – Standards, Vol. 2 | $19.95 |
| 00672479 | Dizzy Gillespie Collection | $19.95 |
| 00673214 | Freddie Hubbard | $14.95 |
| 00672382 | Tom Harrell – Jazz Trumpet | $19.95 |
| 00672363 | Jazz Trumpet Solos | $9.95 |
| 00672506 | Chuck Mangione Collection | $19.95 |
| 00672525 | Arturo Sandoval – Trumpet Evolution | $19.95 |

FOR MORE INFORMATION, SEE YOUR LOCAL MUSIC DEALER, OR WRITE TO:

**HAL•LEONARD®**
**CORPORATION**
7777 W. BLUEMOUND RD. P.O. BOX 13819 MILWAUKEE, WI 53213

Visit our web site for a complete listing of our titles with songlists at
**www.halleonard.com**

Prices and availability subject to change without notice.